Praise for *I Am Hutterite*

"A coming-of-age narrative ... as riveting and well-paced as a novel, with pitch-perfect writing."　　　*—Publishers Weekly*

"Honest, strong, clear, direct, it opens the door on what has been for so many of us a completely closed world."

　　　　　　　　　　　　　　　—Winnipeg Free Press

"A superb memoir that takes us into the hidden heart of a prairie Hutterite colony. In a style both sparing and supple, Mary-Ann Kirkby conjures up both the warmth and simplicity of Hutterite life and the pain of leaving it. This has the makings of a prairie classic."

　　　　　　　　—award jury, Saskatchewan Book Awards

"As one who reads dozens of books per year, I count Kirkby's chronicle of her 1960s-era upbringing in a Hutterite community in southern Manitoba among the most impressive works in recent memory."　　　　—Evelyn C. White, *The Vancouver Sun*

"A yearning to still belong to the thread of life that is trapped in a timeless bubble comes through in a loving voice."

　　　　　　　　　　　　　—Smoky Lake Signal (Alberta)

"A touching story about rediscovering one's birthright."

　　　　　　　—Redlands Daily Facts (Redland, California)

PENGUIN

SECRETS OF A HUTTERITE KITCHEN

MARY-ANN KIRKBY is an award-winning journalist and the bestselling author of *I Am Hutterite: The Fascinating True Story of a Young Woman's Journey to Reclaim Her Heritage.* Her memoir chronicled her childhood experiences growing up on a Hutterite colony in western Canada and the difficult aftermath of leaving her community to forge a new life in the modern world. *I Am Hutterite* won the prize for best non-fiction at the 2007 Saskatchewan Book Awards, and is a valued curriculum option in Canadian schools and universities as a means to build bridges and teach tolerance and understanding of other cultures.

Kirkby is a member of the Canadian Association of Professional Speakers, delighting audiences with her honest and humorous accounts of Hutterite life.

She lives in Prince Albert, Saskatchewan.

Also by Mary-Ann Kirkby

I Am Hutterite

Mary-Ann Kirkby

Secrets

of a

Hutterite

Kitchen

Unveiling the Rituals,
Traditions, and Food of the
Hutterite Culture

PENGUIN

an imprint of Penguin Canada Books Inc., a Penguin Random House Company

Published by the Penguin Group
Penguin Canada Books Inc., 90 Eglinton Avenue East, Suite 700,
Toronto, Ontario, Canada M4P 2Y3

Penguin Group (USA) LLC, 375 Hudson Street, New York, New York 10014, U.S.A.
Penguin Books Ltd, 80 Strand, London WC2R 0RL, England
Penguin Ireland, 25 St Stephen's Green, Dublin 2, Ireland
(a division of Penguin Books Ltd)
Penguin Group (Australia), 707 Collins Street, Melbourne,
Victoria 3008, Australia (a division of Pearson Australia Group Pty Ltd)
Penguin Books India Pvt Ltd, 11 Community Centre,
Panchsheel Park, New Delhi – 110 017, India
Penguin Group (NZ), 67 Apollo Drive, Rosedale, Auckland 0632,
New Zealand (a division of Pearson New Zealand Ltd)
Penguin Books (South Africa) (Pty) Ltd, 24 Sturdee Avenue,
Rosebank, Johannesburg 2196, South Africa

Penguin Books Ltd, Registered Offices: 80 Strand, London WC2R 0RL, England

First published 2014

2 3 4 5 6 7 8 9 10 (WEB)

Copyright © Mary-Ann Kirkby, 2014

Manufactured in Canada.

Library and Archives Canada Cataloguing in Publication
data available upon request to the publisher.
ISBN 978-0-14-318478-2
eBook ISBN 978-0-14-319194-0

Visit the Penguin Canada website at www.penguin.ca

Special and corporate bulk purchase rates available; please see
www.penguin.ca/corporatesales or call 1-800-810-3104, ext. 2477.

To my wonderful
I Am Hutterite readers
who wanted to know:
Could you go back?

CONTENTS

AUTHOR'S NOTE

Hutterites are reluctant subjects. Throughout their bloody history and in every nation they have called home, they have been treated with suspicion, intolerance, and discrimination. More recently, certain North American media have exploited and misrepresented them to such an extent that individual communities have become even more guarded.

It took time and trust for me to be allowed to photograph and record the people in *Secrets of a Hutterite Kitchen*. At their request, names of the women and men and the colonies I visited were changed. Having made this concession, I was deeply touched by the way colony members embraced me and without reservation received me into their homes.

I am a member of the *Schmiedeleut* sect, which was the backdrop for my first book, *I Am Hutterite*. *Secrets of a Hutterite Kitchen* took me on a pilgrimage to my father's people, the more orthodox *Lehrerleut* as well as the moderate *Dariusleut* sects. It is my dream that readers will begin to see Hutterites for who they are, a remarkable culture that has the same human weaknesses, fragilities, beauty, and strengths as the rest of the world.

PROLOGUE

I was born and raised on a Hutterite colony in western Canada. By all accounts, I had a very happy, and in some respects even privileged, childhood.

In 1969 my world was turned upside down when my parents gathered up my seven siblings and me and left the comfort and security of community for life in the mainstream. Overnight we were thrust into a society we did not understand and that did not understand us.

My Hutterite heritage hung over me like an invisible curtain of shame. Sweeping ignorance and prejudice about my culture made a smooth transition impossible.

Throughout my childhood, I had witnessed the suspicious and hostile stares from merchants and locals when we ventured into towns and cities. Clinging tightly to my mother's hand, I felt safe. She seemed so regal among her beehived, miniskirted peers. To my eyes, her flowing, pleated skirts and crisply starched polka-dotted *Tiechel* headscarf gave her an almost majestic air.

After we left the colony, I became desperate to fit in and be accepted. I disposed of everything that would identify me as Hutterite: my accent, my clothing, my hairstyle.

It took years to integrate and decades more to realize that my culture wasn't the problem.

In June 2007, I published my memoir, *I Am Hutterite*. The uniform rejection by the publishing world compelled me to self-publish. When my book was released, it was the first time in our 145-year history in North America that the Hutterite story was available to the mass market. It detailed my childhood at Fairholme Colony, the reason for my family's painful exodus, and the difficult aftermath of adapting to a new culture.

Like a prairie grass fire, *I Am Hutterite* became a national best seller, winning acclaim and awards on both sides of the border.

I was deeply touched by the way ordinary people responded to my story, never more than when I was told about a critically ill woman in Calgary whose dying wish was to read my book and who died clasping it to her bosom.

Hundreds of letters, emails, and gifts poured in from across the country. A Yukon woman sent me a jar of cloudberry jam that she had made as she stirred and thumbed through the pages of my book, unable to put it down. A construction worker from Quebec thanked me with a bottle of vodka. A young man bussed across Winnipeg to attend a book signing and presented me with a Mackintosh Toffee bar after reading that it was a special childhood treat.

Just as eager to read the book were Hutterites themselves. They had never had their lives so intimately chronicled. Some were bitter that I had exposed the dark side of community life, while others embraced the honest way in which I portrayed them.

Mainstream readers of *I Am Hutterite* longed for the sense of community I was blessed with at Fairholme. They were intensely curious about what my life would have been like if my parents hadn't left the colony.

In *Secrets of a Hutterite Kitchen*, I have returned to the language, the food, and the people of my childhood, to the unmistakeable candor, unbridled curiosity, and self-effacing humor of my clan.

Although I haven't lived on a Hutterite colony for over forty years, my journey back has been a journey forward. And what I have discovered is that neither time nor distance can erase the ties that bind us to our cultural heritage.

Introduction

*"Work brings satisfaction to life but a
measure of laziness strengthens the body."*

*This beautiful Haban faience ceramic plate was
handcrafted by Hutterites in the sixteenth century.
It was discovered in a European castle and is on
display in the Hungarian National Museum.*

IT WAS A GORGEOUS early-October day in 1989, and I was
vacationing in Innsbruck, Austria. Honey-colored light streamed
through the bay window of my hotel room as I relished the
pleasure of breakfast in bed—orange juice, coffee, and large,
crusty rolls with an assortment of jams and cheeses. I pinched

a familiar-looking, pale mound, closed my eyes, and popped it in my mouth. *Schmuggi* (pan cheese) had been a much-loved breakfast staple when I was a child at Fairholme Hutterite Colony in western Canada. The stickiness of the cheese was soft and dewy on my tongue, and I waited for the subtle, licorice tang of the caraway seeds.

In the afternoon, the lush smell of apple strudel and espresso hung in the air, luring people to nearby cafés. On my way to surrender to a piece of pastry, I wandered into the core of the Old Town. Everywhere I looked, I recognized traces of my culture, from the cleanliness of the most modest hotels and shops to the red geraniums in the flower boxes and the weathered grandmothers in their pleated skirts and headscarves.

In the public square, a small group of tourists had gathered near a golden gable that framed an ornate balcony glistening in the bright sunlight. I pressed in so I could hear the tour guide explain that it was called *Das Goldenes Dachl* (The Golden Roof) and was decorated with 2,657 gilded copper tiles. Built in 1500 by Archduke Friedrich IV, this important Innsbruck landmark was the residence of Tyrolean sovereigns, and its balcony was a favorite vantage point from which to enjoy special events in the square below.

A few feet away, I spotted a name on a commemorative plaque that made me gasp. "I know him!" I shouted impulsively, prompting the locals to stop and stare. I had stumbled upon a poignant piece of my history and a man so bold that neither beating nor torture nor death could extinguish the vision in his soul. His name was Jacob Hutter.

The Hutterite faith was born in the sixteenth century when the Protestant Reformation was sweeping Europe. Outraged by the power and corruption of the Catholic Church, entire villages started to break away from the predominant religions. Adding fuel to the fire was the invention of the printing press and the translation of the Bible into the vernacular, allowing ordinary people to read and interpret scripture for themselves.

Jacob Hutter was a twenty-eight-year-old Austrian hat maker who traveled extensively through the Puster Valley selling his wares. He first encountered Anabaptists ("to baptize again") in market towns and was captivated by the zeal and strength of their convictions. They argued that infant baptism was an invention of the Catholic Church and that people should be baptized as adults of their own free will. Inspired by the biblical model of the early church in Jerusalem, Hutter led a fledgling group of Anabaptists to a new kind of Christian community, based on the second chapter of Acts, verses 44–45 in the Bible: *And all that believed were together, and had all things in common: and sold their possessions and goods, and parted them to all men as every man had need.*

Hutter's passionate vision of a society where property was shared and people worked together for the common good gave birth to the Hutterite faith and way of life. Their beliefs provoked hatred and intolerance from the church and state, forcing them to flee across Europe. Thousands were arrested and sentenced to death, including Jacob Hutter. On February 25, 1536, he was burned at the stake beneath the gilded copper tiles of the *Das Goldenes Dachl* for refusing to denounce his faith.

His followers found sanctuary in Moravia (present-day Czech Republic), where they established one hundred communal colonies called *Bruderhofs*. They flourished for three decades, pooling their talents and resources, managing farms, dairies, vineyards, breweries, and flour and sawmills. Hutterite doctors served aristocracy, their craftsmen made their carriages, and their scholars taught their children. They excelled as artisans, creating sought-after items such as clocks, wagons, harnesses, saddles, scythes, shoes, hats, lanterns, watches, and cutlery. There wasn't an estate that did not have a valued piece of their merchandise. Most prized was Hutterite pottery. *Haban faience*, with its pure whites and rich blues, was the tableware of choice for lords and nobles. The secret glazing techniques that gave Hutterite ceramics such superior quality were lost when renewed religious persecution forced the Hutterites to flee Moravia and escape over the Carpathian Mountains to Russia. Only 69 of the 30,000 colony members survived.

They lived as a fragmented cluster in Russia for nearly a century. Their finest scholars and artisans had been murdered, their books destroyed, and their way of life shattered. When their military-exemption status was rescinded by the Russian government, they found refuge in the United States. On July 5, 1874, the first wave of 1,200 Hutterites arrived in New York and moved west to settle in the Dakotas. My great-grandfather, Jakob Maendel, was among them.

During World War I, entire Hutterite communities moved to Canada to avoid persecution as conscientious objectors. After the war, realizing their value as land and livestock farmers, the American government invited them back. One-third of them returned to the United States while the rest remained in Canada.

The Hutterite commitment to the common ownership of goods sets them apart from their Anabaptist counterparts—the Amish and Mennonites—and has distinguished them as the finest and most successful example of community life in the modern world. Today 52,500 Hutterites live on 565 colonies in the northwestern United States and on the Canadian prairies.

After their arrival in North America, the Hutterites divided into three distinct sects, *Schmiedeleut* (the most liberal who live in Manitoba, Minnesota, and North and South Dakota), the *Dariusleut* (the moderates who live in British Columbia, Saskatchewan, Alberta, Oregon, Washington, and Montana), and the *Lehrerleut* (the most traditional who live in Alberta, Saskatchewan, and Montana). While liberal communities have significantly altered some traditions such as dress code, and allowed computer access and interaction with the outside world, all three sects share a common language, faith, and food.

I was ten years old when my family left Fairholme Colony and I learned very quickly that my culture had no value in mainstream society. No one seemed to understand that beneath the black hats and polka dots lay rich traditions, a proud heritage, and the best cottage-cheese pie in the world.

Over the past two years, I have returned to the heart of my culture and experienced once again the value of community life. I have sat around polished wooden tables in Hutterite living rooms and dipped crisp chunks of *Recsha Zwieboch* into brimming cups of honeyed *Kreitertee* (herbal tea). I have been serenaded by the a cappella voices of Hutterite women with such perfect pitch and harmonies that it gave me goose bumps. I have laughed until my sides ached, endured inquisitions by four-year-olds, and witnessed the wonder of new birth, the joys of a wedding celebration, and the bitter pain of loss.

I have participated in rituals and traditions that were established in medieval times and have been privy to the inner workings and secrets of the colony kitchen. And I rediscovered what I have always known—it is the women who are the soul of the community, feeding its 100 members three times a day, 365 days a year. They enfolded me into the cycle of women's work, generously sharing the age-old recipes of my childhood.

At my father's home colony in Alberta, I pored over a copy of the archival recipe book that our ancestors brought with them from Russia. Every head cook uses its original recipes—fresh noodle soups, roasted ducks and geese, and irresistible breads and buns. Delicious and wholesome, its menus reflect the food that would have been at hand in early Hutterite communities: flour, butter, eggs, milk, cream, pork, and poultry. Some, like *Schnitz* (dried fruit), were adapted for long journeys over land and sea. Others have been modified, like the *Graua Knedel* (gray dumpling), which the women tie with cheesecloth and put through the spin cycle of the washing machine before cooking.

Hutterite food is an extension of my identity. Bound by an invisible strand, I have been reawakened to its worth in a world where lives are becoming increasingly homogenous and families diminished by the crush of modern technology.

I hope the rituals, traditions, and food of my childhood will nourish you as much as they have nourished me.

Guten Appetit!

Total Colonies

Lehrerleut	157
Dariusleut	195
Schmiedeleut	213
Total	565

Population

Lehrerleut	15,504
Dariusleut	14,972
Schmiedeleut	21,930
Total	52,407

one

The Invitation

"Proud people fall into wells."

Adorable kindergarten children

THE GRAVEL CRUNCHES beneath the tires of my car as it moves past a pasture of bellowing Holstein cattle, their heads sloped skyward. Beyond a well-kept cemetery, I see giant hulks of farm machinery; industrial buildings; cattle, hog, and chicken barns; and a duck pond. The air is thick with grain dust and burning stubble, and a gust of wind pushes me toward a cluster of homes with identical doors. I am looking for a name—*there it is*—Leah & Caleb Mendel.

Leah is the head cook at the Davenport Hutterite Colony, and she has invited me here. I met her only yesterday when I did a reading at the Moose Jaw Public Library near Regina, Saskatchewan. She surprised me by arriving early with platters of butter ball cookies that the women at the colony had baked that morning for those attending. They want to meet me, and she has come to extend the invitation in person.

Like most Hutterite colonies, Davenport is off the beaten path, a safe distance from the temptations of the outside world. That's why I'm nearly an hour late and a degree too hot. But it's not the searing prairie heat that melts my heart. Standing at the bottom of the stairs that lead to Leah's front door are half a dozen small children between the ages of two and six. They squirm and point as I step out of my car.

"*Doh is Sie!* Here she is!" squeals one of the little boys.

"The kindergarten children want to look at you so we let them out early today, but you're late," chides Leah, leaning out her front door.

I crouch down to their level and fall under their spell.

"How's your name?" asks one of the little girls attempting to address me in English. Her bronzed face is the color of honey, a canvas for eyes as blue as the summer sky.

"Mary-Ann," I reply, extending my manicured hand. She looks at my nails and gasps.

"How you git claws like dat!" I raise my *claws* and pretend to pounce. The giggling starts. Some of the children are missing baby teeth, and their innocent, beautiful faces appear so delicious that I could eat them up!

"*Geats hets Hahm.* Go home now," says Leah, gently shooing them. "There won't be enough room in the house when the women come over, and the children have seen you now," she explains.

I wave to the peekers leaning out of neighboring doors who are watching my ascent in four-inch heels.

"My *Gott*, you're going to kill yourself!" yells a woman from three doors down.

By now, I'm used to being scolded about my impractical footwear. I have loved high heels ever since I was a young girl at Fairholme Colony and our glamorous teacher came to school in her black patent pumps. Mrs. Phillipot was hired by Fairholme to teach grades one to eight, but her teaching skills paled in comparison to the education she gave us about the fashions of the outside world. She would leave her shoes in the schoolroom closet, and in the evenings and on weekends, we would try them on and clomp around pretending that we were "English."

My visit coincides with three o'clock *Lunche*—the Hutterite version of high tea—which is eaten in individual homes rather than in the community kitchen. I smile as Leah sweeps me into her house. A large room off the front hall is dominated by a round oak table, a sofa, and kitchen chairs. The walls are bare except for a schoolhouse clock which has pride of place above the sofa.

Women begin to pour in through the front door, and soon the living room is packed with almost forty visitors, including my high-heel heckler, Rosa. They are here to meet the author of *I Am Hutterite*.

"I loved da book," a teenage girl, Naomi, pipes up. "I laughed and cried and wished it wouldn't end."

"*Ich hob ach!* I did too!" exclaims Rosa. "I enjoyed it so much I read it twice."

Leah appears with a pie, holding it in both hands. Her face is Hollywood perfection. Shapely unplucked brows frame olive-green eyes, flushed cheeks, and a self-assured smile. At forty-two, she doesn't have a single gray hair, although she later admits to yanking them out one by one with a pair of drugstore tweezers.

Typical layout of most Hutterite colonies

*Knitting and visiting is
a favorite pastime for women*

Women making cottage-cheese pies for Lunche

She lowers a piece of *Schuten* pie in front of me, and the sparkle in my eyes tells her that the cottage-cheese dessert is one of my favorite indulgences. I am being watched as I sample the creamy, moist slice, and the older women smile, pleased that I remember this old Hutterite staple.

"*Nehm sah ob; ich vil sah on probiern.* Take your shoes off; I want to try them on," Naomi demands. I unbuckle the straps and slip off my heels, as she eases out of her sensible Skechers and forces a socked foot into my left shoe. All the polka-dotted heads tilt toward the floor while Naomi hops around the room, the strap flopping alongside.

"Sit down and put the other one on," I suggest. With so many eyes on her, Naomi is starting to feel self-conscious.

"*Se sei hellisch unmacklich.* They're hellishly uncomfortable," she informs the spectators, swaying while trying to keep her balance.

"*Sue trombleh! Kola Weltleut mit nixs zu toen kinnetn af suwos kumen. Nehm sah ob, Naomi. Kums Lunche.* What an affliction! Only fools with nothing better to do could come up with shoes like that. Take them off, Naomi," a wise, elderly woman sitting next to me commands, putting an end to the shoe show and summing up the collective opinion in the room. I am hastily fitted with a pair of bright orange knitted slippers.

Ninety-three-year-old Miriam Basel is the oldest woman on the colony. She is seated next to me because she is hard of hearing. As a sign of respect, Hutterites call mature women *Basel* (aunt) and men *Vetter* (uncle) regardless of their relationship to the person. The women dote on Miriam Basel and give her a plush cushion for her chair.

"*Ich hob da Dornn Ankela gekennt.* I knew your Dornn grandmother," Miriam Basel tells me, a wad of pie poking her left cheek out. Her eyes glisten as she tells me how well loved my grandmother was. "She shared a cook week with my aunt at Rockport Colony," she adds, jabbing me with her fork.

Leah brings a fresh pot of coffee from the kitchen while I am cross-examined by the other women about my English life, who I'm related to, where I've been, and what I've seen. If curiosity killed the cat, this would be the coroner's office.

There is something magical about this comfortable front room where we alternately laugh, listen, and poke fun at one another. No one is struggling to pay their mortgage, is burdened with childcare, or needs to shop for groceries. There are no cell phones, tweets, or texts interrupting our conversation.

I jump to my feet when I hear the colony bell ring. When the Hutterites came to North America, every colony had a large cast-iron bell on top of the community kitchen that would ring six times a day. The bell would chime fifteen minutes before the main meals to notify the elderly, new mothers, and caregivers of the sick that the food was ready and that they should come and get their portions. This is referred to as "first call." At the top of the hour, the bell would ring again, calling the rest of the community members to the dining hall.

Bells are a throwback to sixteenth-century Europe where they played a central role in religious protocol. Because they invoked painful reminders of our forefathers' persecution, colony bells have never been rung to summon members to church.

When I was a little girl, if my friends and I ever felt the need for a good spanking, we only had to go to the stairwell of the kitchen basement at Fairholme Colony and grab onto the long, thick rope and pull. The powerful upstroke would lift us right off our feet, suspending us briefly in the air. Outside, the bell would chime in time with our swing. The ride was a thrill but its effects in galvanizing the community for naught had undesirable consequences on our behinds.

On many Hutterite colonies, the bell has been replaced with an intercom system in the community kitchen that reaches every home, barn, and shop on the colony. It is also used to transmit the half-hour evening *Gebet* (church) services into homes of those who are too sick or elderly to attend.

The bell informs me that it is almost 5:00 PM and I'm the guest speaker at a fundraising event two hours' drive from the colony. Leah bolts out the door as the other women gather around to say good-bye. Lined faces press their cheeks against mine. My childhood is leaving the room, and I feel melancholy.

Leah reappears carrying five homemade sausages, a bag of fresh buns, and a platter of Hutterite egg fries called *Ahlah Messy*. "I brought you supper from the kitchen. You can eat it on the way."

She hands me the food through my open car window as I settle into the driver's seat. I pluck one of the salty fries from the plate and pop it into my mouth.

"Why don't you come back?" Leah asks softly.

"Oh, I can't, Leah, not tonight. It's too far."

"I don't mean tonight. I mean another time when you can stay a while," she says, patting my shoulder. "Come and work with me and the women in the kitchen for a few days. It will do you good."

Could you go back? That's a question I have been asked over and over again. Crowds at readings and book signings told me that I made them hungry—hungry not only for the pies and pastries, soups and sausages, but for the proficient way of doing things, the camaraderie and the collective wisdom that anchors a communal way of life.

Leah tucks loose strands of her hair into her polka-dotted *Tiechel*.

I hear a rumble in the distance, followed by a loud clap of thunder as I sample one last hot, crispy fry.

"I will," I answer impulsively.

The sky opens and it begins to pour.

- -

LEAH'S BUTTER BALL COOKIES

1 cup brown sugar
1 cup shortening
1 egg
1½ teaspoons baking powder
1 teaspoon vanilla
Pinch of salt
2 cups flour
Granulated sugar
Walnuts

Mix well and mold into golf ball–sized rounds. Roll in granulated sugar and press half a walnut on top of each cookie. Bake in moderate oven at 350°F for 10–15 minutes.

ᶜ⃝ RECIPES

two

The Head Cook

"Guests and fish are
only fresh for three days."

Men and women eat on opposite sides of the dining room,
and the head cook checks that everyone has enough to eat

I HAVE ACCEPTED Leah's invitation. One month later, at ten o'clock on a Tuesday evening, Leah's mother is pacing the floor as I enter her home. She has insisted that I stay at her house for my two-day visit.

Greta Basel has removed her vest, jacket, and headscarf and greets me in her cropped, white blouse and *Kappela* (cap) looking like an angel. Her warm embrace tells me that I'm in good hands.

She shows me to my room with a queen-sized bed along one wall and a twin along the other. They are both covered with brightly patterned feather comforters. A large table sits near the door, chock-full of neatly folded bolts of fabric.

"*Schlof guet und schnell*. Sleep well and fast," Greta Basel tells me as she closes my door.

I slip beneath the comforter. I feel strangely at home here. There is a breeze coming through the open window, and I sleep like a stone until five thirty the next morning when my door swings open and Greta Basel cheerfully announces, "*Steh auf, leg dich on und kum ause*. Get up, get dressed, and come out."

Leah has walked over from next door and is waiting for me in the hall. "Breathe in," she says, as we make our way to the community kitchen in the dark. "It will wake you up." The air is crisp and sharp and feels invigorating. Leah pulls open the heavy doors that carry us into the kitchen, and we are met by a warm draft and the smoky scent of coffee.

The main kitchen leads into the adult dining room where all community members from age fifteen to eighty take their meals. The elderly or those with health issues can have their food brought to them at home, but many seniors still come to the dining room because they enjoy the fellowship. Long wooden tables flanked with benches are set end to end down the right and left margins of the dining room. The men sit on the left side and the women on the right. *Noch die Alter* (according to age) is a common Hutterite saying that describes the seating arrangement. Everyone sits in groupings of their peers. The teenage girls sit together, and across the aisle so do the teenage boys. As you age, you move farther down the row.

Lydia and Ana, the assistant cooks for this week, have already begun preparing breakfast. Thick, creamy oatmeal is bubbling in an oversized crock, and Lydia is setting jugs of milk and containers of brown sugar on carts and wheeling them into the dining room. Ana adds baskets of bread and an assortment of jams to the tables. The mother and daughter pair will be working closely with Leah over the next week, preparing three meals a day for the entire community.

There are five managerial jobs for colony women: head cook, cook for the sick, head seamstress, head gardener, and *Klanaschuel Ankela* (kindergarten grandmother). As head cook, Leah has the most prestigious job, but she is backed by an entrenched and sophisticated system of support. All women from the ages of seventeen to forty-five work in pairs in weekly rotations of cooking, cleaning, and baking. Like the head chef, line cooks, and sous chefs in a hotel kitchen, the head cook and her assistants ensure that the potatoes are peeled, buns are baked, meals are cooked, and everything is served hot and on time.

After the age of forty-five, women move into semi-retirement. They are no longer required to have a cook or bake week or go to the garden, but they still have to wash floors until age fifty, help in the slaughterhouse until age sixty, and do dishes until seventy if their health is good. Most of the older women miss the companionship of their peers and continue to lend a hand with jobs such as peeling potatoes or making noodles. It's a unique and orderly system of sharing the workload.

The head cook creates weekly menus, which are posted every Friday in the community kitchen. Breakfasts range from hearty plates of bacon, eggs, and toast to homemade cheeses, sausages, and fresh bread. The noon and supper meals include traditional favorites like a full rack of lamb, smoked turkey, or *Fleish Krapflen*—pig's brain in a pocket of deep-fried pastry. *Samstich Wurscht* is a special sausage eaten on Saturday, and dinner on Sunday is always fresh noodle soup and stuffed roast duck.

The meals are built around the meat dish, and while Leah also chooses the side dish, such as potatoes, the assistant cooks get to decide how it will be prepared: mashed, baked, or fried. Fresh, canned, or frozen vegetables are served with every meal and so is a light dessert, such as homemade yogurt with canned apricots, cherries, rhubarb, or crabapples.

There is only one cookbook on a Hutterite colony and it belongs to the head cook. Many of Leah's recipes are handwritten; the traditional ones are in beautiful Gothic German text.

In the structured society of colony life, food is one of the ways that women can express their creativity. Along with standard dishes, mainstream recipes have also found their way into the community cookbook. Sometimes, fresh ideas are gleaned from magazines in the doctor's waiting room or are borrowed from other colonies that have already tested unfamiliar cuisine. The newer recipes such as popcorn salad, Chinese stir fry, and pizza have to be adapted to serve a crowd.

Kitchen mishaps are rare, but there are exceptions. A year ago, 600 people nearly went hungry at Triple Pine Colony when a new head cook was preparing food for a funeral. There wasn't room in the main kitchen to finish the 250 pounds of beef needed for the supper meal, so the cook and one of her assistants took the meat and gravy to the stove in the slaughterhouse to let it simmer. Both had assumed that the other had turned down the heat, but when they went to retrieve the beef, all that remained were inedible strips of dry shoe leather. Three vans of men were sent to buy out the local Kentucky Fried Chicken outlet in town, and the poor head cook had to endure the humiliation of being front-page news on the Hutterite grapevine.

Davenport Colony has ninety-eight members, including thirty-five women, thirty-seven men, and thirteen teenagers. Coming together to eat three times a day is compulsory for both adults and children. The sick, the elderly, and new mothers are the exceptions. I join the women's table for breakfast in the community dining room. The coffee is robust, and the bread dreamy—soft as a cloud and as smooth as the butter I spread it with. Leah floats down the aisles wielding a coffee pot and checking to see that everyone has enough to eat. As the meal draws to a close, she hurries in from the kitchen with a square piece of paper. The first woman she hands it to reads it and passes it along. When it reaches me halfway down the row, I'm baffled by what's written on it. *The Indians are coming* is all it says. What's that supposed to mean? I puzzle handing the paper to my neighbor Junya Entz. "Oh." She gestures, reaching for a stack of bread. "Billy Mosquito is coming for the leftovers." Billy, I learn, is from the nearby Indian reserve, and once a month, he comes for the colonies' accumulated leftovers, which the women package and store for him in the colonies' walk-in freezer. While Leah and her two assistants, the *Nochesser* (after-eaters), enjoy their breakfast squirreled away at a corner table of the dining room, the rest of the women wash the dishes and floors, and head downstairs to peel potatoes and carrots for the coming week's dinners and suppers. When I ask Leah why she wrote the note, she tells me, "Because I want the women to prepare some food for Billy. In the past when he came, he was so hungry that he started eating the frozen stuff as soon as he got in the car. Now I get the ladies to fix him something nice and warm."

We return to an immaculate kitchen. Leah looks relaxed and satisfied as she removes her cooking apron and grabs her *Wannick* (jacket) from a hook near the door.

"Come. I'll show you around," she beckons.

Everything in the kitchen is restaurant-sized and made of heavy-duty stainless steel: large braising pans, steam-jacketed kettles, great soup vats, commercial deep fryers, a Bunn coffee machine, and Cleveland skillets that can cook up to seventy-five pounds of ground beef at once.

Leah leads me to the colony's latest acquisition: a Rational oven prized for its consistency and versatility by the professional catering industry. The oven, which uses both dry and moist heat to cook large quantities of food, carries a whopping $55,000 price tag but is the choice of many top-end eateries, including the White House.

Head cook making beef stew

Colony kitchen with a new Rational

Individual refrigerators and freezers are in the community kitchen, not in members' homes

With so many hands on deck, kitchen clean up is very quick

Fresh bread is baked weekly

The potato-peeling caucus, famous for juicy gossip

Absolutely the best pickles!

Women make noodles and dry them with fans

"The Rational cuts down on cooking times," Leah says, adding that the steam heat replaces the need to use fats. Some colony members grumble that they miss the taste of grease, so she alternates between the Rational and skillet frying to ease them into healthier eating.

There are three 10-foot-long, polished stainless-steel tables for food preparation. One is in the center of the room, and two of them are on wheels. A custom-made divided sink the size of a bathtub anchors the south end of the kitchen; one side is for washing dishes and the other is for rinsing. The contrast between the high-tech cooking equipment and the old-fashioned way of doing dishes begs the question "Why don't you get a dishwasher?"

"The women don't want one," answers Leah matter-of-factly. "It takes less time for seven women to wash and dry the dishes than it would for them to pack a dishwasher. "Besides, that's how we find out what's going on in other colonies," she chuckles. In a society that shuns television, radio, and the Internet, the kitchen is the perfect gathering place for a chinwag.

Just off the kitchen, the bakery is filled with tables, cooling racks, shelves of pans and bowls, and a row of built-in ovens. Leah points out the sheeter/molder, an industrial workhorse that can push out thirty loaves of bread dough in a minute. A conveyer belt carries the dough to sheeting rollers, which remove air pockets and eliminate the job of hand kneading. The women on bake week will turn out twenty-five loaves of bread each week as well as 100 dozen buns. Every Wednesday morning, they'll make forty-five pies or cakes to be sent home to individual families; each colony member over six months of age receives half a pie and cake. The baking is enjoyed as an afternoon or evening snack or served when drop-in guests come to visit.

We descend to the basement that houses the cool rooms for storing potatoes, carrots, beets, parsnips, cabbages, and onions. It smells dusky and ripe, like a garden in early September just before the last of the produce is harvested. Outside the storerooms, the women are clustered around three large, round tables stacked with potatoes and carrots. The younger women do the energetic work of hauling and washing the vegetables while the subgroups peel and cut them into chunks. Paring knives fly as practiced hands slice through the peels like butter and, in no time, a growing mound rises from the center of each table. The vegetables are transferred upstairs into a large container of cold water where they will stay until the cook's assistants begin dinner preparation.

As Leah predicted, the chatter is spirited and lively. "I heard that Ida from Twin Oaks finally had her baby, but, shucks, it's another girl, and she has five of them already," Rosa announces. "Two horses died of 'nobody knows' at Golden Valley," says another. Greta Basel, who has joined the table of older women, informs them that eighty-nine-year-old Micah from a nearby colony is on his last legs and that they had better start baking buns for the funeral.

The basement is well lit with stark white walls and polished gray floor tiles. We peek into the furnace and boiler rooms, which rate a tour stop on the merits of cleanliness alone. One end of the basement has been divided into storage for canned goods, jams, jellies, and pickles. *Sauer Kraut* and pickles are considered essentials, indispensable for easing digestion and as a defense against muscle cramps.

"We make absolutely the best pickles," Leah vows, grabbing a gallon jar from a middle shelf so I can reach in and fish one out. "There is very little better than a glass of wine and a pickle in the evening when all the work is done." She sighs. It's a pairing that I haven't tried but I'm already a convert, biting into the crisp, briny dill with just the right amount of vinegar.

Rows and rows of preserves stand like soldiers ready to satisfy the palates of the community throughout the cold winter months ahead: quart jars of green and yellow string beans, crimson beets, bite-sized portions of corn on the cob, golden crabapples, glossy peaches, and dark, sweet cherries swimming in heavy syrup.

"What is this?!" I exclaim when Leah snaps on a bright light as we enter a long hallway next to the storage room. Twenty identical commercial refrigerators and freezers, one for each family, line the walls. Leah opens her fridge marked LCM for Leah and Caleb Mendel.

"We are not allowed to have refrigerators in our own homes like the *Dariusleut* and the *Schmiedeleut* because our elders feel it takes away from a sense of community," she explains. Those such as head cooks who do have a house fridge, must remove the motor and keep food cold with bags of ice retrieved daily from the community kitchen.

Her fridge and freezer are stuffed with cartons of ice cream, frozen pizzas, slabs of cheese, boxed crackers, cookies, potato chips, containers of nuts, jujubes, and cherry sours, chocolate bars, pop of every variety, wieners and sausages, donuts, cakes, licorice, and Cheezies. Candy heaven and waistline hell.

"The colony keeps us supplied with a generous amount of treats," Leah says, stating the obvious. She grabs an Almond Joy and pops one mound into her mouth and hands me the other.

The last stop in the basement is a room with large, oversized cupboards for every household called the *Kamelah* (cool storage rooms). She shows me the shelves for her family that contain a variety of juices, apples, oranges, bananas and more chips, chocolates, and crackers.

We return to the front of the kitchen and peek into a room the size of a walk-in closet. This is the head cook's private domain, but it's not where she comes to relax. It's stocked with dry goods and neatly labeled plastic containers of spices and seasonings. Here she prepares a weekly shopping list for the colony boss who purchases the items in bulk at big box stores in the city.

I trail Leah to the large, walk-in colony freezer past the bakery. We are met with a wall of icy air and are momentarily wrapped in a frigid vapor. Hutterites are carnivores, and the shelves against each wall are stacked with large quantities of freshly butchered meat. Leah keeps a close eye on her meat rations and lets the colony meat cutter know the cuts and quantity to prepare for the week ahead.

Next to the walk-in freezer is an equally large walk-in fridge that stores eggs, buckets of fresh milk and cream, butter, seasonal vegetables, containers of pig and goose lard, and gallons of condiments like ketchup, mayonnaise, and horseradish.

Leah loads her cart with five pounds of chicken feet, twenty fryers, and ten old hens and wheels it out to the kitchen. If meat is king of the Hutterite menu, then soup is the queen, served for Sunday dinners, special occasions, and on cold winter days when a bowl of hearty broth is welcoming and nutritious.

Ask any colony cook the secret to a savory broth and she will tell you: one tough old hen. The succulent, amber stock is the base of traditional soup recipes such as *Geschtel* (noodle nugget soup), *Maultosche* (big cheek soup), and *Nuckela* (dense and buttery dumplings in a transparent stock).

Leah fills the soup vat with water and adds the chicken and a fistful of salt. While the stock simmers, we prepare the *Nuckela* dough. I crack the 110 eggs while Leah weighs soft mounds of butter into a large dish. She tells me that some community members like their dumplings hard and others like them soft. The trick is to use just the right amount of flour for the perfect balance of firmness and texture.

"We also eat a lot of noodle soup," says Leah, pressing and molding the *Nuckela* dough. "Our colony makes homemade noodles every three months, and it takes us a day and a half. We start with eight 30-pound blocks of dough, which need to be very stiff, so we cover it with heavy plastic and the women pack it down by stomping on it with their feet. The over-forty-fives always come to help."

The dough is cut into rectangles the size of a bar of soap before it is flattened in a noodle-making machine that was manufactured on a neighboring colony. The strips are dried overnight on the dining room tables with the help of electric fans. Once dried, they are fed through the machine's cutting head and transformed into fine, angel-hair-sized noodles.

Leah lifts the lid of the soup vat and, as the steam rises and envelops us, I am a ten-year-old girl again watching Ona, the head cook on Fairholme, pull a dipper full of broth from the belly of the vat. Through the mist, Leah passes me her ladle, and as I sip the hot, shimmering liquid, I am transported back to the *Essenschuel* (children's dining room) eating school of my childhood where my love affair with food began.

Leah's Diary

Monday, March 9
5:40 a.m.

The alarm clock goes off, and I groan inwardly. I open one eye and glance around to find the sound, hoping that I set the clock one hour too early and I can crawl back to bed for another half hour or so. I slip out of bed so I don't wake my husband and slowly start to get dressed, brush my teeth, and do everything that goes with morning awakenings.

I plan my day as I walk the short distance to the community kitchen to prepare breakfast. The kitchen is already a bustle of activity when I walk in. My two assistant cooks this week are chopping lettuce for a tossed salad we are having for the noon meal, while other women from the colony are filling thermoses of coffee to take home. Our kitchen coffee machines are like a small Tim Hortons, and any family can bring a thermos to be filled for the colony's 8:30 morning coffee break.

I get out the bowls of *Schmuggi* [homemade pan cheese] and breakfast ham and cut it into slices for each person. I have been head cook for seven years, so by now I know exactly who wants what and how much. Paul and Lydia are the only two who don't like ham at breakfast, so I leave them out. It takes fifteen minutes to cut the ham.

Today, we are having a chicken stew for the noon meal. The chicken breasts that I cut up yesterday afternoon into nugget-sized pieces have to be coated with seasoned flour. We layer the nuggets on baking sheets so they don't stick together and then I put them back in the walk-in fridge until after breakfast. One of the helpers wanders over and asks if I need assistance, which I *always* accept gratefully!

At 7:00 a.m., the adults have breakfast in the community dining room. While they eat, I can go home to see that my family can find everything they need to get dressed, like socks, shoes, and *Tiechel*. I fix my daughter's hair, since she has not quite gotten the hang of *drahing* and braiding. My husband has gone to the community kitchen to have breakfast with the other men, and the children will eat after the adults do.

When I return to the kitchen, my assistants and I have our breakfast. The rule is that the head cook has to bless the food before we eat and give thanks afterwards. I say the prayer for the three of us, and we hurry through our breakfast. Monday is always our busiest day because it's the day I take inventory and make my shopping list for the boss.

∞

7:30 a.m.

I brown the chicken meat that we have rolled in flour and boil the sauce. The recipe calls for a large amount, and it needs time to simmer properly. I add carrots, onions, potatoes, and meat to the sauce, put it into two big pans, and set them into the Rational oven to slowly cook.

∞

8:00 a.m.

With the main dish out of the way, I have a bit of spare time and can go home. My fifteen-year-old son is the assistant to the colony cow man and does the milking early in the morning, so he usually misses breakfast. Otherwise, even if you are not hungry, you still have to show up for the main meals. I'll see what he's in the mood for today. Most days, I'll fry him some eggs and sausage and make some toast. I can see that my husband has made up all the beds, swept the floor, and picked up after the kids. I want to set out my material and patterns for things that I plan to sew this week. I won't do much today, but at least I will get it ready.

∞

8:30 a.m.

It's coffee break, and my husband should be here any minute. He's the colony mechanic, and he always comes home between 8:30 and 8:45 in the morning. The kids also come in from German classes, so whoever didn't eat much for breakfast can have something now: Cornflakes, an apple, or just plain bread and peanut butter. Our break lasts till 9:00 a.m., and, in a flash, everyone is gone again. The children go to English school, and my husband and son go back to work while I tidy the house.

9:15 a.m.

All children under the age of six eat their noon meal at 10:00 a.m. Because they have breakfast at six in the morning, they are hungry by now. They have a bowl of soup and *Totsch* [a cross between a pancake and an omelette] every day, which they love. While the *Totsch* is sizzling on the hot surface of the skillet, I bring out my bacon for breakfast tomorrow. This might seem early, but I have twenty 500-gram packages to fry. I cut them through the middle and separate the pieces before laying them on Combi racks. I move from the bacon to the pea soup that we'll be having for supper to the *Totsch* and back to stirring the chicken stew. Thankfully, my two assistants have their wits about them, lending a hand and taking away dirty saucepans and ladles to be washed. It doesn't take long for me to pile up a lot of dirty dishes. Not all cook's assistants are as helpful as these two. Some slowly wander about, and that makes it much more stressful for me because I constantly have to remind them what needs to be done.

10:00 a.m.

The mothers have come to take food home for their little ones, and the *Klanaschuel* children have also received their share. We are having ginger beef for supper, so I bring out the meat from the fridge to cut into long strips. We'll need to slice almost forty pounds of meat, and one of my helpers comes to assist me as soon as she sees me putting out knives and cutting boards. I glance out the window and see one of the other ladies going home from the laundromat with her freshly washed clothes. Oh, I am so glad mine is washed and folded! I definitely would not have time today.

Individual homes don't have a washer or dryer; each family has its own small wagon to haul laundry baskets to the eight industrial washing machines and dryers just off the community kitchen. In one hour, they can have laundry for a household of twelve washed, dried, and folded. In some colonies, everyone does their laundry on Thursdays with individual wash times posted in the laundromat. Others have alternating days, but our women can use the laundromat as needed. I usually do mine either late at night or bright and early in the morning so it's out of the way when kitchen duty calls. When my alarm goes off, I throw on just enough clothes to run over and start a load and then come back to do my washing up while the washing machine is running through its cycle. I also like to do a load on Sunday evening so that we have fresh laundry at the beginning of the week.

It is close to eleven o'clock, and we are done with the beef strips. The assistant cooks and I sit down to have our dinner and discuss some of the other dishes we will have this week. Usually we allow ourselves fifteen minutes to eat before the kitchen area has to be swept or somebody is on the phone wanting something.

⁂

11:30 a.m.

It's time for the first-call bell to ring. There's a flurry of activity as everybody caring for the ill, the elderly, or the new babies comes to the kitchen for food. People with visitors also have the option of feeding them in their own homes and can come for their share. Everybody brings their own serving dishes from home. The minister also eats at home, but his dishes are supplied and washed in the kitchen. The head cook is in charge of the meat on the menu, so I portion it. Some people have eyes bigger than stomachs, and if everybody helped themselves, nothing would be left for the rest of the colony members!

When everyone has left with their food, we start dishing out for the rest of the people. All the unmarried girls over age fifteen come to the kitchen to set out the food. When the second bell rings, the doors to the homes burst open, and the dining room is full in three minutes flat. I know this because I've timed it. Sometimes I help my assistants wash the pots and pans that we used for cooking, but it's really my job to see that everybody sitting down has enough food. As I refill the empty serving dishes, I get a good idea if the meal is a hit or if it's a recipe that I can throw out. I wish everybody was as easy to feed as I am.

⁂

12:00 noon

What a hectic morning! I have to command myself to put everything down, go home, and put my feet up. I take it one step further, and lie down and read before I drift off for a nice snooze.

1:30 p.m.

My eyes fly open when I realize what time it is. I go to the kitchen and drain the ginger beef of the brine we put on this morning. I putter around doing odds and ends and prepare the sauce for the beef, which the meat will simmer in once it has been browned.

2:15 p.m.

It's time to prepare *Lunche* for my husband and four children. It's the favorite break for colony families. The women rustle up goodies like ice cream, cookies, and chocolate bars from our personal fridges and freezers in the kitchen basement and take them home. Most of us have a real sweet tooth! After our snack, I can cut out a few parts on the white shirts I want to make for the men in my family.

3:45 p.m.

I have to prepare the filling and the dough for the perogies we will have for the noon meal tomorrow. I also have to

make a *Mues* for tomorrow's dessert, and the milk and
cream have to cook on low heat for a whole hour before
I put in the flour and sugar to thicken it. I'll save some of
the liquid to make a separate batch for the members of the
colony on a gluten-free diet. I thicken theirs with special
flour called Celimix.

᛭

5:00 p.m.

It's time for the children under six years old to eat again,
so every mother or her *Lukelah* [babysitter] comes to take
home food for them. When they're gone, the cooks and I
have our supper. I'm in a rush because I need to shower and
change into fresh clothes so I can go to church. It's always
nice to sit and relax. Sometimes my mind will wander and,
instead of hearing the words of God, I am making a menu
for the next week or thinking of ways I could have improved
a certain dish.

᛭

6:15 p.m.

It's suppertime and all I need to do is make sure everybody
has everything they need in the dining area. After supper,
all the women available will stay to make cottage-cheese
perogies. I don't need to help, but I'll stick around to see
that the filling is nice and firm and not too runny. It has
been a long day, and I am ready to go home and put my
feet up until I start to feel guilty—that usually takes about
fifteen minutes!

Retirement Ages for Colony Women

Cooking and baking . . . . 45 years of age
Gardening . . . . 45 years of age
Cleaning the laundromat . . . . 50 years of age
Washing floors . . . . 50 years of age
Making noodles. . . . . 65 years of age
Slaughterhouse work . . . . 60 years of age
Doing dishes. 70 years of age

Rules for Coming Back to Work

Women with Surgeries: Caesarean, Hysterectomy, Gall Stones, Bunions, Ruptures

After 10 weeks . . . . wash dishes, peel potatoes
After 16 weeks . . . . garden, cook, clean, butcher

Tubal Pregnancies, Appendicitis, Small Ruptures

After 7 weeks . . . . wash dishes, peel potatoes
After 10 weeks . . . . garden, cook, clean, butcher

New Mothers

After 8 weeks. . . . . wash dishes, peel potatoes
After 12 weeks . . . . garden, cook, clean, butcher

D & C and Miscarriage

After 2 weeks. . . . . all work

℘ RECIPES

three

Rites of Passage

*"Children thrive when they are
clean, structured, and motivated."*

Klanaschuel Ankela *serving children the noon meal*

"NEM DOSZ TZU DIE KLANASCHUEL. Take this to the
kindergarten," the head cook tells me as she hands me a platter of
Totsch that she has just pulled out of the stove using her apron as
an oven mitt. The crepe-like batter is a cross between a pancake
and an omelette and is often served to young Hutterite children
because it is a good source of protein and easy to digest. Along
with *Totsch*, the head cook has added pickles and warm squares of
ham to the platter.

Annie Kleinsasser is the *Klanaschuel Ankela* (kindergarten grandmother) this week at Emerald Lake Colony, and she watches me from her window as I make my way toward the kindergarten, just a stone's throw from the community kitchen.

It's a cold morning, and the fragrance of egg and ham is familiar and comforting. It seeps up from my serving dish and reminds me of the aromas that used to greet me every morning as I tumbled through the door of the *Klanaschuel* at Fairholme Colony. My favorite breakfast was *Schmont Wacken*, bowls of cream so thick that we could turn them upside down and not lose a drop. The tables were set with baskets of fresh buns, bottles of Rogers Golden corn syrup, and homemade strawberry jam, and we could barely wait for grace to end before plopping generous dollops of syrup or jam into the center of the cream. We'd plunge the soft, fresh buns into the luxurious dip until the bowl was wiped clean. It tasted sensational.

Annie Basel opens the door when I arrive and welcomes me. I pass through a small hallway where black jackets and woolen hats dangle from rows of hooks. The young girls in their beautiful *Mutzen* (bonnets) remind me of the bonnets that my mother used to make, and the painstaking way my surrogate grandmother, Oma, would braid my hair as I sat on the kitchen table. She'd start with tiny braids at the front, weaving them into thick ropes down my back. After twisting my braids into a bun, she would put on my *Mitze*. "*Hetz bist du guet aufgeraumt.* Now you are nice and tidy," she would say, gently cupping my face in her hands.

The children are wriggling in their seats when I set the food down on a nearby counter.

"*Wer bisten du?* Who are you?" a young boy inquires innocently, scratching his right ear.

"*Sie ket tzu uns.* She belongs to us," the kindergarten grandmother tells little Eddy as she fills his cup with fresh milk. Her polka-dotted *Tiechel* frames a friendly, oval face, and her thick body appears custom-made for the comfort and security of young children.

Clean, rested, and well-fed children are a priority on the colony, and they are entrusted to seasoned caregivers like Annie Basel who provide a stable environment for their charges. She is one of three *Klanaschuel Ankelen* voted in by the male members of the community and selected from a roster of women over the age of forty-five. The job is shared on a rotation basis.

My *Klanaschuel Ankelen* at Fairholme Colony were superb storytellers, a valuable skill for those working with children. Every afternoon, Sana Basel held us spellbound, transporting us to the land of Egypt where Joseph's brothers sold him into slavery. With a simple *undt nah* (and then) we were off to Russia for the dramatic fable of *Rass Wa Tri*, the Russian coat maker who outsmarted a pack of ravenous wolves.

The kindergarten at Emerald Lake Colony is brand new, but the layout is much like the one I attended decades ago. It is divided into two parts. The main room is a kitchenette with one long, child-sized table and benches where the children are taking their meal. Next to the main area is the sleeping room with small mattresses lined in neat rows. There is one bigger mattress for the *Klanaschuel Ankela,* who always takes a nap with the children. One side of the sleeping room is for boys, and the other is for girls. There is also a room to play, as well as a fenced playground with a sandbox and swings. Hutterites believe in the benefits of fresh air, and the children love going outside, summer and winter. Often, mothers will stop by and check on their offspring.

"Come look at our new washroom," Annie Basel beckons as she opens the bathroom door. On either side of the adult toilet is a pint-sized urinal and toilet for the children. "It makes them so proud when they can go to the bathroom by themselves," she tells me with satisfaction.

The children are a wide-eyed, curious lot and, by the time their smooth, bare feet stick out of their little blankets in the napping room, they know everything relevant about me: my age, where I live, my marital status, the number of siblings I have,

Young boys' winter hats

Lifelong bonds are forged in the colony Klanaschuel

The Klanaschuel Ankela *with her charges*

Klanaschuel children kneel to say their prayers

*Six- to fourteen-year-old children wait in the eating
school to say a prayer before the meal*

Young girls start to wear a Tiechel *at age six*

The children learn to read and write in Gothic script

*Everyone has a turn to read out
loud in German school*

*At age seventeen, young women start having
a bake week*

where they live and what they do, my son's name and how much I weigh—which is the only thing I lied about.

Four-year-old Evelyna is the lead interrogator. Cute as a kitten, her little mouth purses as she gears up for another question, until Annie Basel finally pries Evelyna's chubby little hand off my forearm and sends all the children off to play.

"The apple doesn't fall far from the tree," Annie Basel shrugs. "Her mother is just as *neisheerich* [nosy] as she is!"

Children attend *Klanaschuel* from age two and a half to six. Unlike a day care center where children often come from wide-ranging lifestyles and value systems, the *Klanaschuel* is a natural extension of the routines and morals that youngsters have at home. This makes it easier for both the child and the caregiver.

Hutterites created kindergartens in the late 1500s when most of Europe was illiterate. They developed a progressive set of guidelines for the training of children, including memorizing catechism, singing, and storytelling. That model is still used in colonies today, and songs and prayers continue to be taught in High German.

When Evelyna and the other children kneel to say their prayers, Annue Basel, hands clasped, stands facing them. The little ones pray with one voice, rocking like babes in arms, back and forth to the implicit tempo of their supplication. I remember so well being one of them.

At two o'clock in the afternoon, the younger tots are collected by their mothers, but the older ones disperse on their own. Young boys seek out their fathers and ride along with them on tractors or run errands in the barns and machine shops. Young girls dash to the community kitchen or down to the garden where their mothers are bent over rows of beans or strawberries.

When I was young, my friends and I would head straight for the pea patch, eating our fill of peas right from the pod. Bellies satisfied, we waddled up the hill to the colony hatchery to visit the new goslings chirping under red heat lamps. We grabbed the squirming newborns in our pea-stained fists until the colony goose man came at us, flailing his arms, forbidding us to touch them. No matter how many times he shooed us away, we always returned.

Die Essenschuel (The Eating School)

It was an immensely happy and secure time in our lives. Lavished with love, we were fed, fostered, and sheltered by an entire community with a vested interest in our well-being.

In the back of the community kitchen, the elevated pitch of children's voices leads me straight into the *Essenschuel* (the eating school), where all those between the ages of six and fourteen take their three main meals. On some colonies, the *Essenschuel* children eat in the adult dining room immediately after the adults have been fed, but here at Beaver Dam Colony, they have their own dining room. The long, wooden tables and benches along the north and south walls are filled with lively children, but when I arrive, most of the attention is on Rebecca Wollman. Today is Rebecca's sixth birthday, and she has graduated from the *Klanaschuel* to the *Essenschuel*, where she is eating for the very first time. Rebecca has been waiting for this moment for the entire year.

At six, children are considered to have a measure of *Verstont* (understanding) and begin an apprenticeship that will instill respect and a sense of duty and responsibility. Small obligations will be put in place at home by Rebecca's mother who might ask her to look after her younger siblings, clean her grandmother's dentures, or fetch the family's share of cakes and pies from the community kitchen. She will take a turn in the *Essenschuel* clearing tables, washing dishes, and sweeping floors, gently easing her into the cycle of women's work. Young boys who turn six begin their apprenticeship with their fathers and uncles, doing small chores in the barns, machine shops, and fields after school and on weekends.

Little Becca has a look of triumph on her face as her indigo eyes dart around the room. When she walked through the community kitchen this morning on her way to the eating school, she was an irresistible target of loving pinches by the older women. The head cook and her assistants made a fuss about her new *Tiecheln,* which is knotted so tightly under her chin that her plump cheeks spill out on both sides. Six months ago, the head seamstress brought her mother enough fabric to make Rebecca three *Tiecheln*—a symbol of Hutterite women for centuries. Exchanging her bonnet for the headscarf marks her ascent from childhood to young girl.

No longer under the care of the *Klanaschuel Ankela,* she is now under the supervision of George Wurz. The German teacher is responsible for religious instruction as well as supervising the children in the *Essenschuel* during the three main meals. Beneath his stern exterior (a requirement for the job), he is soft-spoken and patient and has a good rapport with the children, but his booming voice can quickly bring order to eating school chaos. Some German teachers can be unnecessarily harsh, but that is contrary to the official policy for Hutterite schoolmasters established in the late 1500s. "Those dealing with children must treat them as their own," wrote early scholars of the faith. "Children can be won, trained, and corrected much better with kind words than with severe discipline."

Mainstream curriculum is taught by a teacher from Red Deer who comes to Beaver Dam every weekday and teaches grades one to eight at the colony school. One hour before and one hour after secular school lessons, George Vetter (Uncle George) instructs his students in speaking High German and in reading and writing the language in ancient Gothic calligraphy. Mastering this script is a fine art and takes years of practice to perfect.

In her final year of German school at age fourteen, Rebecca will have written a book by hand, which George Vetter will bind for her at the colony book bindery. The book will include centuries-old Hutterite songs for every occasion, including morning and evening songs, as well as Christmas, Easter, and funeral hymns. Many have up to 105 verses and were written by our forefathers in prison dungeons, a solemn reminder of the price paid for religious freedom.

"*Stilla, mir wenn beten!* Quiet, let's pray!"

George Vetter motions to a young boy, who stands, clasps his hands, and says the German table prayer with lightning speed. Memorization of ancient prayers, catechism, Bible verses, and songs are compulsory, and children are adept at reciting.

While the German school teacher keeps order, the *Essenschuel Ankela* (eating school grandmother), who assists him, ladles out steaming bowls of *Roen soupen* (beet soup.) It is served with thick cream and delicious fragments of fried dough called *Knedel*. The deep burgundy color of the soup stains the children's mouths red, and they look like badly painted figurines. Jars of canned chicken, steamed corn, and fresh bread line the tables, and the children keep the *Essenschuel Ankela* on the run cleaning up spills and refilling soup bowls.

In the *Essenschuel* at Fairholme Colony, my best friend Catherine and I would pick out chunks of beets from our soup bowls and take them home after the meal. We would lock ourselves in my bedroom closet and stain our lips and cheeks a deep crimson. When our mothers called, we would race to the bathroom and scrub our faces, not wanting to be caught emulating loose women from the outside world, at least not publicly.

Prior to age six, Hutterite children are not allowed to attend church, but on their sixth birthday, it becomes compulsory to go to *Gebet*, a half-hour evening service held seven days a week, and to the *Lehr*, a one-hour Sunday morning service. Instead of sitting with her parents, Becca will take her place on the first bench on the women's side of the room with other girls her age. It will be the disapproving glances of the *Prediger* (minister), not her mother or father, who will help her mind.

In addition to her *Tiecheln*, Becca's ascension brings with it two new dresses and the thrill of being one step closer to entering the secret world of Hutterite women. Everyone who pinches her cheeks or cups them in their hands to tell her how proud they are of her reaffirms Becca's increasing value and worth to the community.

Zu Die Leit (To the People)

Zu Die Leit (to the people) is the final rite of passage for Hutterite children, a transition to adulthood that is recognized with a seat in the adult dining room. William has just turned fifteen, and Rhoda Waldner, the head cook at the Washington Colony, has set an extra plate on the men's side of the dining room for him. "Look how *stulz* (proud) William looks in his new bronco hat!" shouts one of the cook's helpers, who watches him make his way toward the kitchen for the noon meal. "He finally ate enough *Knedel* to eat with the grown-ups," chimes the head cook.

Upon turning fifteen, a girl becomes a *Dien* and a boy becomes a *Buah*. The ascension is marked by gifts from the community including hope chests and *Schronken* (wooden dressers) for a girl, made by the colony carpenter, and, for a boy, a straw hat for fieldwork and a new black cowboy hat that will become part of his daily wardrobe to signify that he is now an adult.

In previous generations, boys were given a team of horses to feed and groom, but William will be assigned a tractor or a combine to work the land. He will train in the hog and cow barns, in the machine shop, and in the fields on a rotational basis until he marries and is given a permanent position in the community.

Young Hutterite men eager for a taste of the outside world often find jobs in the mines and oil fields of western Canada and in the northern United States. A strong work ethic combined with a versatile skill set makes them sought-after employees by mainstream companies. "We don't need a resume," William tells me. "All we have to do is tell them we grew up on a Hutterite colony."

Six months ago, when Rhoda's daughter, Sandra, turned fifteen, she also received a *Shronk*. It comes with a lock to give teenagers a measure of privacy to keep cards and trinkets or bottles of perfume or aftershave for date nights. "We all have our little secrets," Rhoda says knowingly.

In addition, young women start learning to sew and will receive fabric for new dresses and blouses. Boys also get material for shirts and pants, which will be sewn by their mothers. In lieu of hats, girls receive a new pair of shoes.

The boss's wife also gave Sandra a rolling pin, a paring knife, a butcher knife, a paintbrush, a waterproof apron, a pail for picking garden produce, and another pail for washing the floors. She now participates in all aspects of women's work except cooking and baking.

"Sandra's over at the carpentry shop with the other girls doing some varnishing today," Rhoda tells me. "She's not that good at it yet, but she will be."

A lazy son or daughter is seen as a shame on the family. Not pulling your load can make young people the subject of gossip or a whisper campaign. Instilling a strong work ethic in their children is the responsibility of the parents.

"It's important for my children to do their part. You don't want them sitting around being idle, that's for sure," Rhoda explains as she folds a basket of towels.

Both William and Sandra are allowed to quit school on their fifteenth birthday. In their early history, Hutterites were leaders in education, and even children of the nobility attended their schools. Education was compulsory for females as well as males. This practice of educating women was adopted only two hundred years later by Hapsburg empress Maria Theresa.

But by the time Hutterite ancestors reached the Russian Ukraine in the early eighteenth century, their scholars and artisans had been annihilated due to intense and persistent persecution. The surviving sixty-nine families were a mere shadow of the people they once were. They would have starved to death were it not for Johannes Cornies, a wealthy Mennonite landowner from Molotschna who took pity on them. Cornies was a government agent, and he found the Hutterites land, taught them how to farm, and helped them establish their own schools; practices he had to fight to retain here in North America.

In an effort to revive the scholarly tradition of the Hutterite fore-fathers, the more progressive Hutterites push for higher education, and both men and women from the Schmiedeleut sect earn teaching certificates from universities and return to teach at colony schools. But the traditional sects such as Beaver Dam are strong proponents of apprenticeship, believing that teaching by doing is the way to go.

Back in the dining room, William retrieves his bronco from the hat rack and heads out to the fields to work with the men. He is excited about his future and already has his eye on a girl from a neighboring colony. Even without a high school education, the training he will receive in the next few years could lead to a number of managerial positions on the colony, including the most prestigious job of colony minister.

A *Prediger* is the spiritual head of the community. He is chosen by lot, and his job is set for life. He conducts baptisms, funerals, marriages, and daily church services, but unlike ministers and priests in the outside world, he does double duty as a laborer and might serve as the colony beekeeper or the smokehouse manager.

His executive consists of the *Wiet* (financial manager or boss), who pays the bills and manages the books, and the *Weinzedel* (farm manager), charged with daily job assignments to all the young men fifteen and over. The minister meets with the farm and financial managers every morning along with two or three *Zullbrueder*, respected senior men on the colony. Together, they make decisions that range from day-to-day operations to disciplinary matters. After marriage, men are elected to positions such as cow or hog man, field boss, mechanic, or electrician.

For now, William will heed the advice that the German teacher gave him on his last day in the *Essenschuel*. "Just remember," said Jacob Vetter, "you are just as good as everyone else, but you're no better."

Bake Week

The warm, yeasty scent of fresh bread pulls me toward the colony bakery. As I round the corner, a teenage girl is removing her white apron. To her left, dozens of white and whole wheat loaves are cooling on racks. "How did they turn out?" I ask her.

"Just perfect," Frieda beams, swinging her hands toward the racks.

The composed teen turned seventeen on Monday, and by Wednesday she baked fifty-two dozen buns for the first time. Today's job was sixty loaves of bread.

"I wasn't nervous, just excited," she gushes. Her mother, Clara, is her baking partner, and her lips curve into a perceptive smile, tiny beads of sweat visible on her forehead.

"We push them out of the nest right away, but of course we watch out for them. Every mother wants her daughter to bake great buns!" she admits.

The pair arrived in the bakery at 4:15 a.m. so colony members could have fresh baking for the 8:30 a.m. coffee break.

"Do they always turn out this well?" I ask, offering my services as a taste tester. The large, crusty loaves are a deep golden color.

Frieda cuts off an end piece, butters it, and passes it to me. "Most of the time they do," Clara says, "but a year ago I was touring the bakery with some English ladies from town. Laura, one of our best bakers, was shaping the loaves, and the English women wanted her secret to making good bread because they always buy it at our farmers' markets in town and just love it. She boasted that her bread always turned out because she put in more effort than some of the others. Laura told them a long and wide story of how some of our women are on the lazy side when it comes to baking." Clara demonstrates, extending her arms. "Well, you wouldn't believe it! Her bread flopped that day, and poor Laura was so ashamed she didn't show up for the noon meal. So I told my Frieda, 'The secret to making good bread is don't brag!'"

Leah's Diary

Tuesday, April 21
5:30 a.m.

Today I'm not even thinking of catching a few extra winks because I need my time this morning. I dress quietly and quickly, and as soon as I get to the kitchen, I fry the bacon. I have to do this in four batches to fit the baking racks. It takes eleven minutes to cook each batch. Just before 7:00 a.m., my assistants fry the eggs for breakfast. I put the bacon into serving dishes while they do the same with the eggs. We ring the bell for the adults. The adults usually eat from 7:00 to 7:15 a.m. As soon as they are finished, the women will clear the tables, and the children aged six to fourteen will be waiting in the wings to have their breakfast. They have to be in German school by 7:30 a.m., so we are very prompt in the kitchen.

7:30 a.m.

I can go home for a few hours, but I occasionally phone to the kitchen and ask my assistants to check the pork ribs in the Rational. At 10:00 a.m., I hear the bell ringing, announcing that the food for the younger ones is ready. Today, my assistants can handle breakfast for the children, and I'll have another half hour before I put everything down and go back to the kitchen. I'm making good progress cutting out my shirts as I have taught myself not to dawdle around too much. If I'm really pressed for time, I will not even take time to answer my home phone.

10:30 a.m.

The first thing I do in the kitchen is take out the chilled *Mues*
I made yesterday. It is a delicious dish with a raisin and prune
fruit bottom. It's a bit like custard, but creamier and not
as firm. I put one at each place setting in the dining room,
then go back to baste the ribs with homemade barbecue
sauce. I always get an opinion from my assistants on whether
anything has too much spice or needs more. Some are really
helpful in offering ideas, but others try getting through the
week as easily and quickly as possible. I guess cooking is not
for everybody. It's 11:00 a.m., and today the cooks eat first.

<hr />

11:30 a.m.

First call, so once again I dish out food for the little ones
and those taking food home. When they're all gone, I start
dishing up for the rest of the colony. Today has not been
terribly busy, but who could take a whole week of Mondays!

<hr />

1:30 p.m.

I'm going back to the kitchen. My assistants have gone home,
and I can do little chores in a relaxed way. Tomorrow my
assistants will bake cinnamon rolls. We make pastries and
pies every Wednesday. It's the head cook's duty to prepare
and mix the filling. I get out the large mixing bowl and
weigh out all the ingredients. I go downstairs to my storage
Kamelah and bring up the cereal for breakfast tomorrow.
This week it's Rice Krispies. Everybody seems to love them,

and those who don't can take them home and give them to someone who does. There are leftovers in the walk-in fridge for those who don't want cereal, and there's always milk, eggs, and bread in the kitchen. Nobody needs to be hungry, as we can take things to make ourselves something at home.

3:30 p.m.

Today we are having pizza pretzels, coleslaw, and a chunk of homemade sausage for supper. My assistants have kneaded the dough, and it's time to shape the pretzels so they can rise. I am in charge of measuring out the cheese and pizza sauce that I have ordered from the boss. I'm already starting to wonder what we could have for dinner next Monday when the new week starts. Seems early but, with the large amounts of meat solidly frozen in the freezer, I like to put it into the walk-in fridge so it's nicely thawed by Sunday. All week long I'm organizing a menu for the next week, and I admit I have times when my mind is a total blank. Other times I feel so creative, I can make menus for three weeks in advance. Sometimes we'll get good recipes from a bag of rice or a package of coconut. I often ask my assistants for help, and some are very good and come up with wonderful suggestions.

Wednesday, April 22
6:00 a.m.

Today, there are so many women in the kitchen and the bakery that we get in each other's way. Not only are my

assistants there, but women on bake week and their helpers
are rolling out the dough, adding the filling, and making
the icing for the cinnamon rolls. My assistants are tending
to the whole ducks that have to be boiled and crisped
for the noon meal. I put a bowl of Rice Krispies at each
place setting in the dining room, remembering to heap up
Daniel's and Levi's bowls on the men's side because they
seem to have hollow legs and can't get enough. My assistants
will get the milk out of the fridge just before breakfast so it's
nice and cold. We also serve fresh bread and butter, honey,
and strawberry jam, which have already been set out on
the tables.

I can hear the kitchen phone ringing, and somebody is
calling my name. That means my family is coming to life at
home. A small voice over the phone asks, "Mom, how come
I can't find my socks? Where did you put my shirt?"

"If you can't find it in your drawer, just wait and I'll be
there shortly," I always say. Most of the time they're wearing
the missing item when I get there, but it makes me feel good
to know they still want to hear Mom's voice.

7:30 a.m.

Breakfast is over, and the cinnamon rolls are baked and
cooling. The women have started to frost them. I measure
out the dry ingredients for pancakes for tomorrow's
breakfast. As soon as I'm done, I will start giving each
family its share of frosted cinnamon rolls. We bake our pies,
cakes, and cinnamon rolls on nine-inch pie plates, and each
person, no matter how young or how old, receives a half-
pie portion. Of course, we had to make gluten-free ones

for five members of the colony, but their pastries are never as soft and fluffy as the ones we make with wheat flour. I always hand out the baking by 8:30 so everybody can enjoy it with their morning coffee break. I grab my share and go home to enjoy them with my husband and children. I'll still have some time to do a bit of sewing. The shirts I cut out on Monday need only snaps, since I sew late into the evenings. I always have some sort of project started in my sewing room.

10:30 a.m.

A head cook has to be organized, and I like having a handle on everything before breakfast. Today we are having roast duck for the noon meal. I get out the *Geschtel* [noodle nuggets] for the soup. If I have enough time, I will put the seasonings on the beefsteaks that we'll have for dinner tomorrow. At 11:00 a.m., my assistants and I will stop what we're doing and have our own dinner, which is a hurried affair as usual.

I give my storage and spice room its weekly wash today because it gets dusty so fast. I put all the cupboards in order and wash and wipe all my containers. There is always some spillage when my assistants do things in a rush.

1:30 p.m.

Dinner went smoothly and I've had my little nap, so I'm back in the kitchen to putter around a bit. I was able to season the beefsteaks before lunch but had no time for the pork chops we will be having tomorrow, so I will season those now. I like doing this a day beforehand so they're nicely thawed. By the time I'm done and everything is put away, it's time for *Lunche* with my family. We still have cinnamon rolls from this morning, and I'll get ice cream and some Oh Henry! chocolate bars from my *Kamelah*.

3:30 p.m.

We are having square fries, lentil soup, and baked ham for supper. I will cut up the hams, and my assistants are preparing the soup. They laid out all the ingredients before the noon meal. That is usually my job, but I want to prepare the pancake batter for breakfast tomorrow. We think pancakes are much fluffier if the batter sits overnight.

When it's time for first call, I dole out everyone's share before my assistants and I have our supper. Then I must go home to prepare for church. I'm also responsible for freezing the buns and the bread once they've been baked and putting them in the freezer. I have to remember to give the bread time to thaw so it can be enjoyed at mealtimes. Of course, I'm only human, and there are times that I forget and we have to rush around at the last minute. But I have done well this week, so no need to feel bad yet.

four

Field to Table

"When you feel weak, eat cabbage."

Women on the way to the garden in the Wieberwogen
(women's wagon)

I'M AT THE HEAD GARDENER'S house at Misty Acres Colony in Saskatchewan, and I can't stop eating. I have just asked for a third helping of *Gascha*, and Justina Waldner is more than happy to oblige.

Gascha is a Hutterite soup made with fresh garden potatoes and onions simmered in sausage broth. It's served with thick lengths of sausage that the colony made a week ago, and the broth is so savory that I am lulled into second and third helpings. I feel a pleasant pop every time my teeth pierce the skin of the sausage and its salty juices flood my taste buds.

"Who knows what kind of *Tronk* [slop] you eat in your English life," Justina scolds, pleased with my excess. "You're probably full of fillers from all da store-bought food you buy. You're like a *Osche-breckel* [piece of driftwood on the ocean] in dat big, old world out dere!"

I smile at her sweeping generalization sweetened by her charming accent. All Hutterites speak an ancient Tyrolean dialect called *Hutterisch*. Some, like Justina, find the *th* sound impossible to pronounce.

Justina has been the head gardener at Misty Acres for twenty-five years, and her husband, James, is her assistant. "When dey vote in a gardener, da husband is part of da deal. He gets trone in for good measure, a two-for-one special." Justina laughs.

I follow Justina to the garden on the outskirts of the colony where the women are bent over thirty-foot-long rows of green and yellow beans, carrots, squash, beets, onions, cucumbers, broccoli, cabbage, cauliflower, and tomatoes. The vegetable plot is a lush paradise of healthy vines and plants, and the satisfaction in Justina's voice is as big as her garden. "You can almost watch it grow," she coos.

Misty Acres Colony has five acres of garden, but they only seed two and a half acres each year. The remainder lies fallow, and James sows the unplanted land with oats. Just before it starts to shoot, he'll plow it under as mulch.

Seeding begins the first week of May. Justina's husband prepares the soil with the cultivator before most of the seeds are put in the ground with the tractor. The women help with the broccoli, cauliflower, and onions, which are sown by hand.

"Our black soil is rich and can hold moisture better dan sandy soil," she explains as she ushers me from patch to patch.

Cucumbers, squash, green beans, and carrots are planted on the twenty-second of May each year, rain or shine, when the soil has warmed and the last danger of frost is past. Justina likes to sow the carrots late in the spring so they don't become too large or hollow, especially if they need to be stored for winter use.

There are three patches of corn and eight rows to each patch, with enough space for a tractor to maneuver on both sides of each section. Planting the crop in smaller blocks assists with pollination and cuts down on the long walk out of the rows at harvest time.

Corn is a favorite with colony members, so three varieties are sown to satisfy cravings year round. Golden and tender, early cobs are picked fresh, boiled, and served hot with plenty of salt and butter. Sheba is a midseason hybrid with straight, cylindrical ears good for canning. The harvest is extended with a late-season Super Sweet variety that takes about eighty days to mature. They are worth the wait, Justina tells me, but are subject to early frosts, so late harvests are always a gamble.

Some colonies have large market gardens and greenhouses and sell produce to major grocery chains. Two nearby colonies have contracts to provide the local IGA and Co-op food stores with beets and carrots throughout the year, but Justina's colony plants only what it will need to feed its members; leftover produce is sold to the public onsite at local markets or is donated to food banks. Potatoes are the exception, she tells me. "We always overdo it on da potatoes because dats one ting we never want to run out of."

"Our colony could get by wit half a ton of potatoes a year but we plant tree-quarters of a ton because you never know what kind of year you'll have."

Dry years yield fewer potatoes that are smaller; wet years ensure a bumper crop with plenty to store. "We like Norland," she adds, "because it's a good keeper."

They also plant two patches of peas: one for the kitchen and one for the children. "Dat way, if da kids accidentally pull out a vine, you don't have to git heesterical about it," she says practically. Youngsters are encouraged to graze right from the vines. Not only is it a healthy snack, children develop fine motor skills when they peel and shell the vegetables.

Justina places her seed catalogue order from Stokes in Ontario in January. The service is prompt, and they never substitute seed, critical when you are relying on homegrown produce to feed a community of one hundred, she claims.

Last year, she ordered more than 4,000 bean seeds, half a pound of beet seeds, and 1,000 seeds each of Mighty Joe head lettuce and Regal spinach. Three varieties of cucumbers are planted for pickles and for slicing, and she orders as many as 10,000 carrot seeds and 5,000 radishes. There are 2,000 cauliflower seeds and another 1,000 of broccoli, as well as 10,000 cabbages that find their way into soups and coleslaws. Prolific producers like zucchini and squash are limited to one package each, as well as one package of cantaloupe, loved for its cannonball-sized fruit and thick, sweet, orange flesh.

As in most colonies, a section of the garden is devoted to strawberries, raspberries, and saskatoons, ideal for making crisps, jams, or pies. Some years, when the yields are abundant, they will invite other colonies to come and share the bounty. The young women make a day of it, and the head cook provides a picnic-style dinner for them to enjoy under the shade of a nearby tree.

What the colony can't grow, they'll purchase from orchards in British Columbia and Washington State. Crabapple trees in backyards of private homes have also caught the eye of enterprising Hutterites who realize that many homeowners are too busy or unable to harvest the fruit themselves.

"Last fall our girls got arrested," Justina tells me. "Someone called 911 and said dat a bunch of women wearing polka dots were crawling up da neighbor's tree and stealing apples. Da girls were hauled off to da police station. Can you imagine? Dey told da cops dey were friends wit Dr. Wilson, da owner of da tree and dat he told dem to come anytime and pick dose apples. But da cops didn't believe dem until dey phoned Dr. Wilson and he gave them officers da beans!" the triumphant gardener crows. "Den dey realized dere mistake and let our girls go."

Two weeks after the misunderstanding, a red-faced staff sergeant took possession of five, freshly baked crabapple pies from the colony.

At Misty Acres, all women under the age of fifty are required to help seed, weed, and harvest, although on some colonies the young boys are assigned the job. Hoeing starts in June, first with the peas, followed by lettuce, spinach, and radishes. Diligently working the soil destroys weeds, but it also reduces insect damage and the need for pesticides.

"John Vetter, da old gardener, told me 'don't work your land in August because dat's when da cutworms lay der eggs,'" Justina relates. "If da ground is hard and not cultivated, dey don't touch it."

In addition to giving the colony children a jar each and having them remove insects from plants by hand, a job they take to with glee because they are rewarded one candy per bug, the colony tries to employ other organic gardening practices. James sprays the plants with a mixture of water and liquid dish detergent, which doesn't harm the plants but is an effective bug deterrent. "One year, we used bubble bat from Amway," says Justina effusively. "Our garden smelled wonderful, and Gordie Howe we sure didn't have to coax da women to da garden dat year! But it cost too much, so we had to switch to something less expensive," she says pulling a thistle from a nearby row.

Enriching the soil with calcium plays a big role in plant health and keeps insects at bay, but too much can harden the ground, she cautions; you have to know how much to apply.

Much of the garden produce is eaten fresh for summer meals; the rest is frozen or canned and stored on the shelves of the colony pantry. Crop yields can vary from colony to colony, so if one has a shortage of tomatoes or cucumbers, the others will pitch in and offer what they can.

Misty Acres will process 250 jars each of peas and corn; 100 jars of canned tomatoes; 150 jars each of sour beets and string beans; 100 jars of tomato and corn relish; and four kinds of pickles. For fruit, they'll can 200 jars each of pears, peaches, crabapples, apricots, and saskatoons, and 50 jars of black currant mush for freezer jam.

By the end of the growing season, there will be twenty-five 15-pound bags each of green beans, beets, and broccoli. Five-gallon ice cream pails are also used to freeze fruits and vegetables, including ten pails each of peas, corn, and beans; twenty-five pails of strawberries, raspberries, peaches, and plums; fifteen pails of peach, apple, and apricot fruit sauce; and twenty pails each of strawberry, raspberry, and black currant jams.

Justina's twenty-five-year stint as head gardener has allowed her plenty of opportunity to philosophize on the secrets of growing and tending nature's bounty. "Give da children a jar and da women a hoe," she says as we head back to the kitchen for coffee and some Queen Elizabeth cake.

On my next visit to Misty Acres it's late August, and I join the women standing around a great stainless-steel table in the cannery, peeling and cutting meaty red tomatoes. We're being entertained by a senior woman visiting from a neighboring colony whose storytelling abilities and comedic timing have us in stitches. We have just laughed our way through bottling 100 jars of tomato soup when Sonia Basel finishes us off by telling us about Rutha *Ankela* (grandmother).

At eighty-two years of age, *Ankela* didn't have to work anymore, but she missed the companionship of the women and couldn't resist joining in, at least until the latest gossip was spilled and the newest romances debated.

That day, the women were canning peaches, and there was very little *Ankela* loved better than peaches. Besides, her new dentures were bothering her, and she needed a distraction. When the bell rang, she grabbed her favorite knife and made her way to the kitchen basement. The Washington peaches were as big as baseballs that year. *Ankela* took out her top teeth and placed them on her lap. She bit into the sweet, sticky flesh, her eyes squeezed tight with pleasure and juice running down her chin. The women brought her bowls of peaches to peel and halve, and she lasted until the afternoon, when she made her way back home for a nap. It was the next morning before she realized that her dentures were missing.

The manhunt to find them went into full force—women pulled out all the drawers, lifted pots and pans, and checked beneath the stoves and steamers in search of her choppers. But nothing. And *Ankela* was secretly glad to be rid of them. They were new and painful, and she was resigned to the fact that she did not need uppers to enjoy a meal. What was better than bread, *Milich Geschtel* milk nugget soup, and a daily half glass of chokecherry wine?

By late fall, the minister had approved the purchase of a replacement set, but no amount of coaxing could get her back to the denturist. "Well, alright then," said the *Prediger*. "Leave *Ankela* alone. If she's happy, we should be happy too."

The following winter when the snow was swirling outside, the head cook decided to treat the community to a taste of summer. That's when she found *Ankela's* dentures floating in a gallon jar of canned peaches in the basement pantry. Shaking with laughter, she presented the jar to *Ankela* at the noon meal. Equally amused, *Ankela* took it home and placed it on her night table, where it remained until she died three years later. That's when the jar was opened, and the uppers were given to the undertaker. *Ankela* went to Heaven with "canned teeth" that didn't hurt anymore.

"It's darn hard to have three meals a day with someone you have a grudge against," Gideon Kleinsassar confesses. "You really have to be somewhat of a forgiving person to live on a colony." People from the English world are often surprised by the blunt, matter-of-fact manner of Hutterites. In a closed society where people must get along, a candid opinion is considered a necessity; talking around an issue is a waste of time.

Gideon is the field boss at Red Clover Colony, and we are driving in his dusty pickup to look at the crops. The colony's 13,000 acres are seeded in Durham and spring wheat, barley, canola, and field peas for silage. "People think we have a lot of land, but it works out to about 1,000 acres per family."

Like most colonies, Red Clover engages in large-scale agriculture practices. They raise hogs and beef cattle for their own consumption and run a successful chicken operation for commercial markets. Red Clover buys its birds from a hatchery in Saskatoon. "Every eight weeks, we get 10,000 day-old chicks," Gideon explains. "If they hatch in the morning, we're there to pick them up in the afternoon, and we put them on our own feed right away because it's better quality."

When the chickens weigh three to four pounds, they are butchered and sold. It takes from eight in the morning to one o'clock in the afternoon to slaughter, eviscerate, chill, and package 1,200 chickens. Some of the birds are packaged whole, and the rest are cut up and boxed for thigh meat, breast meat, and wings. There is a high demand for their product, and nothing is wasted; even gizzards and feet are sold to Asian restaurants.

Red Clover also butchers old hens, ducks, geese, turkeys, pork, and beef for use in the community kitchen. Every spring and autumn, the task of sausage making falls to Gideon's brother, Ewald, who has managed the colony smokehouse for seventeen years.

"We have a two-cart smokehouse," he tells me as we tour a converted eight-by-ten-foot metal granary filled with two large wooden carts built by the young men on the colony. "Normally, a smokehouse will hold 700 pounds of sausage per cart, but in our smokehouse we can double that. We can do 1,400 pounds."

The smokehouse has been insulated and can take heat up to 280 degrees Fahrenheit. Temperature is critical. If the room is too hot, the fat in the sausages will melt and ooze from the casings. Fat is a binding agent and adds flavor; too little means sausages are dry and crumbly.

Today Ewald is making *Samstich Wurscht* (Saturday sausage). He begins with cold smoke, which is sent through an exhaust fan in the ceiling. After fifteen minutes, the sausages are cooled briefly with cold water from an overhead sprinkler system, and then he turns on the hot smoke. Ewald sets it at 80 degrees Fahrenheit and increases it by five degrees every half hour until the temperature reaches about 110 degrees. The smoked sausage will be cooled with ice water and put in a cooler overnight.

"Lots of guys want my secret," he admits, "but I tell them all smokehouses are not the same. It's like an oven. The timing and the temperature are very precise. You really have to take the size of the room into consideration and fine-tune your technique."

While personal computers in homes are prohibited, they are a welcome addition to the colony farming operations. The teenage boys have installed a computer system for Ewald, and every meat has a code that triggers the heating and cooling times. Still, he opens the smokehouse twice during the smoking process and checks the temperature probe manually.

Red Clover Colony makes liver, summer, and blood sausages, but the favorite is *Samstich Wurscht*, which is served every weekend. They make 2,000 pounds of Saturday sausage a year. "We only use the shoulders and hindquarters of the cow," Ewald says. "One steer gives us 400 pounds of meat. We never use the fat on the beef because we find that the sausage gets rancid faster, but pork fat works really well as long as the pig is skinned."

He smokes fish as well as hams, both which are first rubbed with a half inch of salt and left to sit in brine for a month. At Christmas, he'll smoke 300 turkeys and 600 chickens for holiday meals on the colony and to sell to the public. Last year, the demand exceeded the supply.

As we emerge from the smokehouse, Ewald spots a diminutive figure disappearing into a white building near the duck pond. "That's Light Bulb Joe, our wine steward." Ewald points as we move toward the structure. Most colonies have a wine steward who makes red, white, and blush varieties from any number of fruits, including rhubarb, cherries, dandelions, raspberries, black currants, chokecherries, and Concord grapes. Every family is given a gallon of wine per month, but he also supplies wine for special occasions like *Hulbas* (engagements) and weddings, holidays, and the birth of a child. Joe is a master at his craft, and other colonies lacking his expertise bring their fruit to him so he can make their wine too. In exchange, they will donate an extra truckload of fruit to Joe's colony.

The minute he opens the door, I understand why they called him Light Bulb Joe. He has a bulbous pear-shaped nose that's a twenty-five-watt shade of red. "Have a good look," he says completely at ease. "I've had it since 1937, and it hasn't burnt out yet." His earthy sense of humor is as much a part of his character as his straw hat and suspenders.

*Young boys and girls often help
with seeding in colony greenhouses*

*Working together brings
an abundant harvest*

*Many hands make light work;
women canning tomatoes*

*Off to spray the garden
with bubblebath*

Traditionally, Hutterites are not fish eaters, but in recent years fish has become a healthy meat alternative. Jobs like cleaning fish are often given to the senior men who shoulder a lighter but meaningful workload.

Assistant cook rings colony bell announcing noon meal

Slaughterhouse crew having breakfast

Joe's nose is more than decorative; it's useful. A batch of blackberry wine is fermenting, and the room is filled with a sticky haze that smells of plums, oak, and tannin. "Blackberry is an ancient fruit," he says. "Our ancestors grew them in vineyards in Moravia."

His magic ratio is three pounds of fruit to three pounds of sugar and one gallon of water. He'll use 700 pounds of fruit at a time, which ferments in three stainless-steel commercial milk tanks. The mix is stirred daily for two weeks, and then the fruit is left to settle so the liquid will clear.

"Nothing, nothing," he says emphatically when I ask him what additives he uses. "I don't use any additives or clearing agents whatsoever."

Some wines like rhubarb and chokecherry age for up to ten years, but fruit wines like pear and apricot are ready to drink in a few weeks. "Orlando Colony lets its batches sit too long, and it tastes worse than sewer cleaner," Joe says unabashedly.

The seventy-four-year-old winemaker says his best wines are chokecherry and blackberry. He leads me to a wall of wooden barrels and fills a tin cup with purple elixir. Before handing it to me, he holds it aloft and announces, "Hutterite wine makes you see double and feel single!"

The Slaughterhouse: Plucking Ducks

I am fast asleep on a cloud of soft white feathers. Bright sunlight seeps through an open window, and billows of down float hypnotically around the room. A sudden draft blows the plumes wildly in the air, but I am lost in slumber, as helpless as a rag doll in a blinding snowstorm.

A loud clang rouses me from my feathery dream. It's the kitchen bell. I untangle myself from the luxury goose-down duvet on Katya Basel's king-sized bed.

The whole colony has been up since 5:00 a.m. slaughtering ducks and I'm supposed to be helping, but the truth is I can't keep up. Ever since I started on this journey, I am in awe at the ease with which both men and women do so much physical work in a single day. I enjoy the camaraderie of it all, the potato peeling, the bun rolling, the gardening, and most of all the gossip and banter, but the pace is killing me.

Last night as Katya Basel tucked me into her bed, claiming the guest bedroom for herself, she insisted that I sleep in until breakfast. Her daughter Christina, who is on cook week, agreed, telling me she'd ring the bell at 7:00 a.m. just for me personally because, on days that they slaughter, they deliver breakfast to the work crew, so there would be no other reason to ring the breakfast bell.

I thought she was kidding! I jump out of bed flattered and embarrassed to have earned such favor.

Yesterday when I arrived at Pleasant Valley, I voiced my delight that the colony still had a bell. Many colonies have abandoned theirs for a recording or an intercom system, but a kitchen bell is something that will always remind me of my happy childhood at Fairholme.

Samuel, the colony boss, told me an interesting story. Two years ago, a man came to the community and asked their minister if he could inspect the bell. "He didn't say what he was looking for, but our minister said sure. Our boys even got him a ladder. After a while he came down and asked where we got that bell.

"Our minister told him we bought it from someone who told us it came from a burnt-down church. He even showed the guy our bill of sale.

"'That's a stolen bell,' the man told us. He was a representative of the Roman Catholic Church, and he said the bell had been taken from one of their churches. He had the serial number to prove it.

"Well, that kinda shook us up," said Samuel. "But the man offered us a fair compromise. He said if the colony would let him have the bell, he would replace it with another one. And he did.

This one doesn't have the rich deep sounds of our old bell, but it's an honest deal and it does the job." He shrugged.

A year after Pleasant Valley lost its old bell, they suffered a greater loss: the much-loved colony minister. Chris Vetter died while planting peas in the colony garden. That afternoon he was to have attended the funeral of a friend at another colony. He was Katya Basel's husband, and last night we stayed up until midnight talking about him.

I dress and dash to the kitchen. The head cook and Christina are bent over the skillet cracking eggs.

I am greeted with one of my mother's old mantras: "Good morning, merry sunshine, what makes you wake so soon? You frightened all the little stars and shone away the moon," the women all chant.

I knew I wasn't going to get away without some ribbing.

The kitchen help is filling breakfast buns with eggs, cheese, and crisp slices of bacon. As soon as a tray is full, Christina and her cooking partner, Marianne, run them over to a long table set up just outside the slaughterhouse. The buns are being devoured by the hungry crew as fast as they are delivered. Young men are sitting against the building, and older ones are standing with their rubber boots and aprons still on. The women are delving in too, chatting noisily and sipping coffee on nearby benches.

Katya Basel is in the thick of it, her round body energetic and her cheerful face dewy and rosy from exertion. I give her a hug, and she grabs my hand.

"Yo, mah lieba, Mary-Ann. Du host kanna orbetshent. Se sein anfocht zu waach. My dear Mary-Ann," she says, stroking the palm of my hand. "You don't have working hands, my girl. They are much too soft."

"I'm afraid if I came back to the colony, I wouldn't make the team," I admit, disappointed in myself.

"We were just talking about you this morning, and we decided if you come back, we would make you the Klanaschuel

Ankela. You're a good storyteller, you're good with children, and you can have a nap every afternoon when they do," says one of the women from the far end of the table.

"When can I start?" I cry, delighted with the posting.

"We don't always work this hard," a middle-aged woman jumps in. She is standing against the wall, her white hair at odds with her youthful face. "We work hard in spurts, but then we have quite a bit of free time, especially in winters. And the older ones can all work at their own pace. They don't have to come to work, but most of them do."

"Except Lizzie Basel," laughs a teenage girl. "She quit coming to peel potatoes two weeks ago because she said the only reason she ever came was for the *Katuffelschel Gschichtlen* (potato-peel gossip), but she can't hear well anymore, so she said, what is the point?"

When the men disappear into the slaughterhouse, the women set down their cups and plates and follow.

I feel as if I have entered a time capsule. The smell of wet feathers, the slick floors, and the vapor rising from the steam racks is at once familiar.

Raising ducks and geese is a colony tradition. Poultry has been the meat of choice for the Hutterite palate as far back as our beginnings in sixteenth-century Europe.

When I lived in Fairholme, my colony produced ninety-five percent of the geese sold in Manitoba. Other colonies led the way with ducks. Each year my community raised and butchered 20,000 geese for market.

Pleasant Valley raises and butchers geese and ducks just for their own use. Yesterday they butchered a raft of 622 domestic Pekin ducks and today 750. By noon, everything will be done.

The slaughterhouse is equipped with industrial hydraulic and aerial conveyor belts, steam tanks, evisceration vacuums, cooling tubs, and an experienced and seasoned workforce.

Everybody seems to know their place, and everything is done swiftly and competently. Young boys with energetic limbs do the running. They bring the ducks from the chopping block to where they are hot steamed, ten birds at a time for exactly two minutes. From there, the ducks are slung onto wooden tables, lined on either side with young people who strip them by hand of their down at impossible speeds. By the time the next round of birds is on deck, the down from the previous ones has been emptied into large crates beneath the table.

Once plucked of their feathers, the ducks are handed off to the foreman, who dips them into a tub of hot wax and then into a drum of ice water to seal the wax. This eases the removal of the pin feathers. The runners carry the ducks over to Katya Basel's table of senior women. They rub and pluck and tweeze the birds to salon perfection.

A husband and wife team cut open and mechanically eviscerate the ducks with greater efficiency than the twenty women who once did the job manually. The ducks are then passed on to a table of young marrieds who remove what the eviscerating machine has missed and give them a final inspection. Lisa Wipf is squeezed in with the other women. She is as round as a barrel and ready to go into labor at any minute.

"What are *you* doing here?" I scold, imagining myself taking full advantage of an advanced pregnancy and staying home with my feet up.

"I come and go as I please," she says, pretending to throw a gizzard at me and causing a gale of laughter when I protectively raise my arms. Pregnant women are expected to monitor themselves and work according to their ability. Most, like Lisa, with healthy pregnancies do whatever work they feel capable of until going into labor.

During the yearly week-long slaughter at Fairholme, the community always enlisted eligible young men from other colonies to help, and there was never a shortage of interested parties because Fairholme was teeming with beautiful women. I remember it as the most romantic time of year. The teasing and flirting that went on between the unmarried male and female workers was tangible and created a lot of excitement. As children, we were only allowed on the periphery of the operation, but even from there, we witnessed the stolen glances, surreptitious flirtations, and flushed faces of the young women.

But what really took the enterprise to a whole new level was the singing. Through the hot steam and floating feathers would come the most beautiful harmonies as the entire workforce joined in, male and female, young and old alike. Someone would start a religious hymn like "How Great Thou Art," and it would be followed by a couple of German classics like "*Gott Ist Die Liebe*." After a time, the romantically inclined would break into George Jones or Dolly Parton favorites. The singing had an uplifting effect on everyone, elevating what could arguably have been a day of unpleasant labor to a joyful experience.

And here it was again, at Pleasant Valley Colony. From the far corner where the young men and women are stripping the ducks of feathers, someone with a rich baritone voice begins to sing Bette Midler's "The Rose," and he is soon joined by a chorus of young voices. Goose bumps rise on my arms as I take in the pure a cappella sounds.

Singing together when working is standard procedure on most Hutterite colonies; whether butchering, canning, cleaning, or gardening, it is an ingrained part of the culture. Our Hutterite ancestors sang as they were burned at the stake for their religious convictions, and many of the songs still sung by colony people were written by them.

I have been trying to catch up with Billy Vetter, and suddenly there he is in the shadow of the back door listening, as enchanted as I am.

Billy Vetter is the goose man (and the duck man) who has been running from pillar to post in a pair of navy blue overalls and black *Katus* (homemade hat with visor).

As soon as the singing stops, he's off and halfway to the goose barn by the time I catch up with him. Big burlap sacks filled with duck down that he has obtained from the chambers beneath the plucking-crew tables obscure most of his face as we walk. He walks in double-fast small strides, and I have to put in some effort to keep up with him.

When we enter the barn, Billy Vetter empties the sacks in the enclosure where he keeps the young goslings and ducklings when they first come into his care.

He is a short, soft-spoken man with a fleshy nose and kind blue eyes.

"I'm crowding eighty-one. I could retire, but I do this job for my health. I love it," Billy Vetter says, taking big handfuls of feathers and scattering them beneath the heat lamps to dry. "Our buyer will come for them in November after we kill our geese, but first I have to give our women their share. They prefer goose feathers, and so does the buyer." He smiles coyly knowing to whom he owes his allegiance.

The feathers take me back to early-autumn days in Fairholme when I was between the ages of seven and eight, and our mothers used to harness my cousin Sandra and me with a *Federsock* (feather sacks) after school and send us to the far side of the colony to pick feathers. We had to hoist ourselves over the goose fence and pick feathers that had been shed by the thousands of honking geese in our midst.

We found lucrative little handfuls of feathers along the fence line where they clustered, but Sandra, whom I adored, was equally unenthused with the assignment. In an effort to finish the job as quickly as possible, we would add leaves and sticks to our *Federsock*. When we came into view of the colony houses, our sacks bulging, we would be commended by the women looking out their windows or passing us by. The flattery was short-lived once our mothers discovered our deceit.

Sandra and I made a habit of scavenging the bushes on the margins of the geese fields for dead geese because they afforded us a big endowment of feathers on the spot and just the ones our mothers wanted, namely the soft down on the geese's bellies. But a dead goose was a rarity except when Roland, the colony bad boy, showed up. He was as desperate to get into any kind of trouble as we were to fill our sacks and be done.

Roland always seemed to find us when we were at our wits end, red faced, windblown, and with hardly anything in our *Federsock*. Only once did we succumb to his continual offers to kill a goose for us, but the trauma from all the quacking and snorting that took place while we turned our backs and Roland did his dirty deed was more than we could handle. It was hard to tell who was slaying who, because the goose was not going down without a fight. The ensuing guilt far outlasted the thrill, and the prospect of getting caught and being punished was too risky. We went back to grumbling, and Roland went on to commit offenses for those with smaller consciences.

Billy Vetter continues. "Our buyer gives us five dollars a pound for duck and seven dollars a pound for goose feathers. We'll get around 400 pounds of feathers from our ducks," he predicts, shaking loose a large white globe of plumes from between his hands. "The down is shipped to Ontario where it's used to make winter jackets," he adds.

There's a little coffeepot on a corner table next to half a bag of Christie Maple Leaf Cookies. "I make myself at home here," he says, digging into the bag for a cookie and offering me one.

I ask Billy Vetter the secret to raising such beautiful fowl. "You have to work with nature," he tells me.

"You've got to have water if you want to raise good ducks. Geese graze more, but the ducks need water. You want your geese to be content. That way, you will have a healthy bird and good-quality feathers. We feed them grain we grow ourselves.

"It takes longer to raise geese," Billy Vetter goes on. "The ducks we can raise in twelve weeks, but the geese take until the fall. We want our ducks between five and seven pounds and our geese between eleven and twelve pounds."

We make our way outside and are standing alongside the fence overlooking Billy Vetter's flock of geese.

"For seventeen years I was the colony foreman in charge of giving our young boys work assignments, and then I was colony boss for twenty years," Billy Vetter confides.

"In 1992 I took sick and had two big operations, one on my bowels and one on my hips, so I had to give up my position. I was laid up for a couple of years but, thank the good Lord, I recovered, and I've been the goose man now for twenty years," he says pensively. "Being goose man is a great retirement job for me," he adds.

The fact that Billy Vetter was once colony boss and key financial decision maker in what is essentially a multimillion-dollar operation and is now the goose man appears to have been a seamless transition. His interest in the well-being of his community has not diminished nor have his efforts to help it succeed.

He knows the bigger picture as well as he knows his ducks and geese. "We have 600 sows, 500 cattle, 900 sheep, and 15,000 acres sown in canola, wheat, barley, and oats," he tells me as we walk back to the slaughterhouse.

"You've got to have work for your young people," Billy Vetter insists, reprising his role as colony foreman. "If you don't have meaningful work for them, they are far more likely to go astray. You have to make them feel needed. Keeping young people busy gives them schooling and builds self-esteem. It's just like a horse. You can't break in a horse if you've got no work for him, and you can't build a man if you don't have work for him either. You can't raise people and not have work for them. You've just got to have something meaningful for them to do."

"But how do you inspire your young people to do the work you have for them?" I ask. "How do you build a strong work ethic?"

"You have to work *with* them," he says plainly. "The foreman has to work with his crew. It's not like the outside world where you say to your employee, you do that and you do this, and if they don't do it you fire them. We can't fire our young people. We have to work with them to find them a job that suits them. We like to give them an all-round work experience, but in the end, if a boy has a knack for fixing things, we'll put him to the machine shop, but if he's good with animals, we'll get him in with the cow or the sheep man. You have to say come, not go."

"*Arbeit macht es Leben süsz.* Work makes life sweet," says Billy Vetter looking me squarely in the face. "Don't you know that?" he laughs, reminding me of the oft-quoted Hutterite saying.

"Yes, I do!" I nod, having heard it a thousand times from my own parents.

When we get to the slaughterhouse, Billy Vetter pats me on the shoulder and veers off for more feathers. It's almost noon, and the butchering is done. The ducks are in the cooling tank's icy waters, and a full-scale cleanup of the slaughterhouse is under way. The older women have taken their leave, as has Lisa. The men are washing down the floors and walls with pressure hoses, and the remaining women are tackling the steamers and receptacles with pails of soapy water and disinfectant.

I hear the kitchen bell ringing first call and, in true Billy Vetter style, I dash off. The smell of something roasting draws me into the heart of the kitchen where head cook Betty Waldner is dishing out bowls of *Maultosche* (big cheek soup) for the first callers standing around the kitchen island with their bowls and dishes. She fills their platters with thick slabs of roast goose, mashed potatoes, green beans, and a garden salad with young onions and fresh dill.

Betty has a presence as large as her physique. Her buxom hips swing as she moves around the kitchen island dishing out servings of the noon meal for the *Lukelah* (baby holders) and caregivers. She is genial and attentive, especially with the young girls whom she instructs to carry their soup pails away from their bodies so they won't burn themselves if they spill.

She turns to check on the racks of geese that are roasting in the large oven and spreading a provocative aroma in the kitchen.

"A goose is a lot drier than duck meat, so it has to be cooked with more water and steam," Betty says, poking one of the breasts with a fork. "I cut the geese in half lengthwise so I have twenty-four halves per meal. Our geese are much bigger than our ducks, and we need twelve geese per meal. I salt them really well and put them into a large roasting pan half-filled with water and cut-up onions. I cover them with a tight lid and leave them in the oven for five hours at 350 degrees Fahrenheit. Then I pour half the water off for soup, which is a must when serving goose or duck because the broth is so delicious. I leave an inch of water in the bottom of the pan and put the geese back in the oven for half an hour to crisp them. The most important thing is not to dry out the meat.

"With ducks, it's a different story," she says, closing the oven door and blowing a strand of hair out of her face. "We have them every Sunday and need twenty ducks per meal. I place them in a large kettle of hot water with carrots and onion and let them simmer for two and a half hours, which is just about the time it takes to give me a good soup stock. Then I take the ducks out and lay them on large cookie sheets. I salt them thoroughly before putting them into the Rational oven, where they steam heat for another hour at 189 degrees. At 10:00 a.m. I switch the steam to hot air for half an hour so the ducks get nice and crisp. Our church service is over at ten-thirty and we eat the noon meal at quarter to eleven. Everybody is hungry by then because we have only a light breakfast of coffee and a muffin on Sunday mornings," says Betty, splashing gravy over the mashed potatoes on the first callers' serving dishes.

"Too bad you weren't here last week," the head cook declares with a devilish twinkle in her eye. "We serve goose on Wednesdays and duck on Sundays, but last Wednesday we had goose heads instead."

"You don't still eat those?" I recoil, remembering how my mom used to rave about how good they were.

"Absolutely, our community loves them," she says with aplomb. All the first callers nod in agreement.

Unprompted, Betty launches into how she prepares them. "I cook them in water with lots of onions and salt, and as they boil I remove all the foamy scum that rises to the surface until it is absolutely clear. Goose heads render a very concentrated broth, so I always make a nice soup with this meal as well," Betty adds, garnishing everyone's serving dish with two large pickles.

"When we butcher our geese, we leave at least two inches of neck stem on each goose head so it provides a nice serving of meat," she says, illustrating the length with the thumb and forefinger of her left hand. "The tastiest morsels are underneath the cheek and chin areas, but the real prize is the brain. We pry the goose head open with knives and spoon it out. It tastes very delicate, like … umm …" She snaps her fingers searching for a word.

"Does it taste like pâté?" I prompt.

"Not at all," she says, shaking her head. "It has a similar texture, but it's milder. It's very subtle."

"It tastes like lobster," shouts an older woman from a far corner of the kitchen.

"Hutterite lobster," Betty agrees, bobbing her head.

The dinner bell rings, and the first callers disperse while the rest of the community starts filing into the kitchen. One of the women grabs my arm and invites me to sit at her table for the noon meal. We wait while the unmarrieds stream in with platters of food. Once everyone is seated, the colony boss says the table prayer and we all dig in. Eating is done quietly and quickly. Unlike the spirited interactions during work or coffee breaks in people's homes, socializing while eating in the dining room is kept to a minimum. The average time between the blessing and the closing prayer, when everyone is expected to be finished eating and clear the dining room, is fifteen minutes on most Hutterite colonies.

My appetite returns despite the goose-head setback. I have eaten my share of poultry hearts and gizzards, walkers and talkers (chicken feet and necks) when I lived on the colony and even afterwards, but goose heads on my colony went out during my mother's era.

I delve into my bowl of *Maultosche*—two big, cheeky pouches swimming in hot broth. It consists of dough pockets stuffed with a blend of coarse bread crumbs, beaten eggs, creamed butter, and onions. Richly satisfying, it is the perfect reward for a community that has done a day's work in one morning and a marvelous jog down memory lane for me. Thanks to my Hutterite upbringing, I remain on good terms with all things buttery.

The goose meat tastes like home. Though I don't have the opportunity to eat it very often, its intense, rich flavor is warm and familiar. In mid-chew, I catch sight of Billy Vetter across the aisle, contentedly gnawing on a drumstick.

"It's the favorite meat of older Hutterites, so I serve goose at least once a week," the head cook told me. "Our younger generation prefers duck, but we always take the preferences of our older members into account. They have a traditional palate and aren't as keen on the more modern recipes that my young assistant cooks like to come up with. I try to find a nice balance."

I can't keep pace with eating any more than I can with working. When the closing prayer is said, the women swoop in to clear the tables with such proficiency I take my half-finished plate over to the *Nochesser* table where the head cook and her helpers are sitting down to their meal. "I'm afraid I'll end up in the sink with the dishes," I tell them as I slide in next to the head cook.

"That is quite possible," she chortles.

Betty appears custom-made for the job of head cook, but she balks when I tell her so.

"Oh, I didn't want to be head cook," she says emphatically. "My husband really had to promise that he will help me. He sat me down and read me a few persuasive Bible verses to prop me up. I told him I'll cry if I want to, but I knew I had no choice but to take the job."

"Why didn't you turn it down?"

"You can't just decline. You have to have a good reason to say no, and I didn't have one. I was thirty-six years old, so I was at a good age to take the position."

"What if you'd had another baby?"

"If a head cook has a baby, she gets half a year off instead of just the sixteen weeks the other women get."

"How did you get the job?"

"The men vote us in," she sighs. "They go to the church where they all get a piece of paper and pen, and they write down who they want as head cook. Traditionally the boss's wife is appointed head cook, but sometimes as in our colony she's too elderly, so it goes to a vote and whoever gets the most votes gets the position."

The women on dishwashing duty have gathered at our table. Some sit down with us, and others are standing behind listening to the conversation.

"Do you tell your husbands who to vote for?" I ask, seizing the opportunity.

"Of course!" Two of the women immediately respond.

"A man knows who can cook well and who can't. They know who puts good food on the table and who doesn't and who puts a lot of effort into their cook week and who doesn't," an older woman with a yellow dishrag in her hand interjects.

"Yes, but the women want someone they can get along with," insists Marianne, one of the assistant cooks. "Someone who is fair and even-tempered can learn to be a good cook. If you're a great cook but have a bad personality, it affects the whole community."

"I'm an outdoor person. I love gardening," says Betty, unmoved by the compliments. "Plus, I like variety, so I'd rather have a cook week and then rotate like the other women instead of having to be the head cook all the time."

"You'll get over it," says Christina, patting her arm and refilling her coffee cup.

Pleasant Valley Colony Meat Chart—
Requirements per Meal

Ducks	20
Geese	12
Geese heads	60 pounds
Beef ribs	48 pounds
Beef steak	35 pounds
Beef roast	43 pounds or 3 large roasts
Pork ribs, smoked	48 pounds
Pork chops	40 pounds
Pork roast	4 roasts
Pork spare ribs	120 pounds
Turkey (cut up)	35 pounds
Sheep	5 roasts
Sheep chops	50 pounds
Fried chicken	27 pounds (needs two bags)
Chicken breasts	25 pounds
Fish fillets	17 pounds
Fleish Krapflen	18 pounds
Samstich Wurscht	22 pounds

five

Celebrations

*"It's better to give with a warm hand
than a cold one."*

*A young couple's wedding photo, with the woman
wearing a traditional blue bridal dress.*

Weihnachten (Christmas)

It is bitterly cold at Springville Colony in Alberta. I have joined
the potato caucus, and after a morning of peeling vegetables, the
women are off to the colony school to see how the Christmas
concert is shaping up. The concert has generated as much
excitement as the Academy Awards, and the expectations are high

for the thirty students in grades one to eight whose singing still needs some work.

We arrive unannounced, but the two English school teachers are gracious when the women ask for a command performance. The teachers line up the students who are most agreeable to the interruption at the front of the class and lead them in an a cappella version of "O Tannenbaum." The song has potential but clearly needs some polish, and Lena goes effortlessly from lead potato peeler to professional music critic.

"Da children are off-key and should sing louder," she announces, not hiding her disappointment.

"I *know*," says the English school teacher, Mrs. Harder. "But if you would just allow us to get back to work, we will iron out the creases by the twenty-second."

"Okay, okay." Lena nods hopefully, motioning for us to leave.

Preparations for Christmas got under way on the colony in late November when the women baked 4,800 cookies. There were four different varieties, including modern favorites such as chocolate chip and ginger snap.

"We always have to make *Weinachts litszitle* for Zeke Vetter," says Lena, "because he likes our old recipes." Zeke is the colony's eighty-seven-year-old broom maker who loves the chewy, biscuit-colored discs. Infused with anise seeds and a subtle hint of cardamom, these traditional Christmas cookies can be baked and stored in airtight containers and left to ripen for several weeks, but they are equally delicious right out of the oven.

All the holiday cookies are cooled and then packaged in plastic bags or recycled ice cream pails before being distributed to the community. Every household gets one dozen of each variety for every member of the family. A family of eight would receive thirty-two dozen cookies.

While most Christians in North America are dining on turkey and cranberries for Christmas dinner, the Springville feast will include noodle soup, roast goose with stuffing and mashed potatoes, corn, *Brennig-Kraut* (braised *Sauer Kraut* in a cream sauce), and fresh buns and pickles, accompanied by a glass of chokecherry wine for the adults. Dessert is a special treat of waffles with stewed strawberries and freshly whipped cream.

Gifts of food and wine are given at Christmas, but expensive gift exchanges are not part of the culture. The highlight for most members is the customary gift from the community called *Weihnachtsgeschenk,* a yearly extravaganza into the taste-bud wonders of the outside world.

Orders are placed with wholesalers in July, and just before Christmas the boss and his wife go to town to collect a half-ton truck full of store-bought treats. Boxes and containers of dates, figs, nuts, cookies, chocolate bars, assorted crackers, hard candy, gum, Christmas oranges, grapes, apples, and pop are brought to the community kitchen to be divided by the women under the supervision of the head cook and distributed to families. It does not matter whether you've just sprung from the womb or you are halfway to the Promised Land; each member gets an equal share of goods.

"We used to exclude babies until they turned two, but our women decided it's better to just count them in right away. The family can share the baby's portion with friends and relatives if it's too much," the boss's wife, Elsie, tells me, adding that the women also have input into decisions about what should be purchased. Last year, Lena fell in love with Big Turk chocolate bars and brought an empty wrapper to the boss as a reminder to include them in next year's order.

This year, each family receives one pound of hard candy, forty-eight chocolate bars, ten packages of gum, and a jar of Cheez Whiz per person. The parcel also includes generous quantities of cookies and pastries like Twinkies, Wagon Wheels, Oreo Cakesters, Paulins Chocolate Puffs, assorted crackers and potato chips, and Cheezies. Six large boxes of Rice Krispies and cornflakes are assigned per family, a popular night snack for children. Each family also receives four pounds of sugar and four large tins of ground Maxwell House coffee.

No one is as excited by this annual windfall as the colony children. I remember impatiently waiting with my friends outside the community kitchen in Fairholme, our cheeks as red as McIntosh apples and our little hearts thumping. When the doors finally opened, the community dining hall had sprung mounds of candy the size of the Alberta foothills. The head cook and the women had portioned out individual shares and labeled pieces of cardboard with each family's initials. Ours was marked RMD, Ronald Mary Dornn. We eagerly pushed, pulled, and dragged our loads home, but my parents kept a firm hand on our windfall. Everything was stored in the locked *Kamelah,* a cool storage cellar beneath our house, but every afternoon at three o'clock *Lunche* it was unlocked, and we received offerings of cookies, chocolates, fruits, nuts, and sweets.

It's at just such a *Lunche* that I meet the head cook's six-year-old son, Charlie.

"What would you like for Christmas?" I ask over piles of candy wrappers, peanut shells, and orange peels littering the table.

"Nothing I can think of," he replies meaningfully. His straight blond hair is cut short, and his black clothing makes him look like a little professor.

"Oh, come on, Charlie," I prod, poking him in the elbow. "What if I would buy you anything you want. What would you ask for?"

Charlie takes a bite of his Mars bar and chews slowly as he considers my question. "If you give me a present, I'll be happy, but if you don't, I'll still be happy," the young philosopher king replies.

Hutterites don't watch television and Charlie hasn't been subjected to the hype and advertising that children succumb to in the outside world. And neither are his parents in a tailspin about what to buy him, or if they can afford it. Video games, iPods, Xboxes, movies, and cell phones are forbidden, so the wants and needs of children like Charlie are simple, and parents aren't slaves to media influences.

There are no Christmas trees or decorations on the colony, but the season brings its own spirit of excitement without the emotional and financial strain of holiday shopping. Christmas Eve at Springville will be a quiet celebration where extended families gather in the evening for a special *Lunche* and to exchange small gifts. Everyone brings goodies from their community fridges and freezers, but the head cook also provides ingredients for the women to make trays of sausage and cheese and dips for crackers.

A week later, I am back for the Christmas concert, and there is standing room only in the small schoolroom. The concert is being held at four o'clock so the men from the community can leave their farm chores and attend as well. As we file in, the children are in costume and waiting on stage: kings in foil crowns, shepherds with heads wrapped in red bandannas, and white-robed angels with butterfly wings. The spectacle of the children in costume is a unique thrill for the adults, and the children are equally excited to wear outfits supplied by the English school teacher and to play a role so unlike their everyday lives.

As I squeeze into my seat, I can see Lena perched in the front row, her head bobbing left and right, drinking in every detail. At center stage is Mary, as still as a painting, with a pale blue cloth draped over her head and a baby doll in her arms. Just like school Christmas concerts in mainstream society, it's the children's foibles and missteps that provide the most memorable moments.

One of the feathery ends of an angel wing is tickling the face of a little boy in a sheep costume, and despite his best efforts, he sneezes, and the concert begins. Not a minute into it, and a shepherd holding a lit candle accidentally sets one of the sheep's ears on fire. Lena bolts from her seat and claps out the flame with her bare hands. Despite a lingering odor of burned wool, the performance carries on. The singing is still a little off-key, but the audience is delighted; no one minds when tails rip, wings break, and baby Jesus falls off Mary's lap.

The concert ends with gifts from the teachers to all the students. The young girls receive dollar-store dolls, and the older ones are given mint-green ceramic bird figurines, which they will use as decoration in their bedrooms. The young boys are given Weasel Balls, and the older ones receive nodding-head toy dogs. The women also give gifts to the teachers, who are loaded down with jars of canned pears and peaches, pickles, jams, relishes, and two fat frozen chickens.

As we spill into the cold December air, the succulent aroma of roasting pork draws everyone to the community kitchen. Springville Colony has only one potluck a year, and it takes place immediately after the Christmas concert. The teachers and superintendents of the school are all invited and, just for today, the formal seating arrangements are abandoned. Children and adults eat together, and everyone can sit wherever and with whomever they want.

A long table has been set with baskets of fresh buns, platters of pork, *Schuten Krapflen* (deep-fried cottage-cheese pockets), buttered peas and carrots, beets in honey sauce, *Sauer Kraut*, pickles, brownies, and ice cream.

Everyone dives in as soon as the prayer has been said. The Christmas concert has chins at all the tables wagging, but the sheep's scorched ear is getting the most mileage. Lena is thrilled with her command performance as a fire extinguisher.

When I ask Ben Walter, the colony minister, how he enjoyed the program, his answer surprises me. "I didn't," he blurts. "Dere is too much cackling and foolishness, and I tink it's unchristian." As *Prediger*, he tried putting a stop to Christmas concerts at his colony, but the plan backfired.

"I got on da wrong side of da women wit dat notion, and you can't run a colony when da women are unhappy. Dey say da men are da head of a colony, but I tell you da women are da neck and da neck turns da head!" Wise leaders like *Prediger* Walter realize that small compromises and happy women are worth the investment.

Usten (Easter)

It's early April, and the trees are wearing their first flush of green as I walk toward the minister's house at South End Colony. I'm here to celebrate Easter—the most sacred holiday of the year.

A tall, heavy-set man leaning on a cane greets me at the door.

"How are you, Peter Vetter?" I ask him.

"No bad, not boiling," he answers with a sparkle in his fading blue eyes.

"*Votar,* bring *sa eini!* Father, bring her in!" the *Prediger*'s wife shouts impatiently from the kitchenette. We turn the corner, and the table is set for the noon meal. Ministers do not eat with the rest of the community in the dining hall. The assistant minister eats his meals at the home of the head minister so the two can discuss business and deal with disciplinary matters that crop up in the community. Though he has the authority, a good *Prediger* will rarely make a decision by himself.

The assistant minister is away today but Edna Basel is in high gear, plugging in the kettle, setting a basket of buns on the table, and ladling out noodle soup from a pot in the middle of the table. "Welcome here," she says, shaking my hand and looking me over carefully. Our heart-shaped faces look like book ends. "I'm related to you. We're cousins," she informs me, pulling out my chair. "When we were little girls, your mom and I played together."

Peter Vetter says the table prayer, and his amen is as booming as the engine of a 747. Edna Basel jumps up and down like a Jack-in-the-box, relieving her cupboards of crackers, chocolate bars, and cookies to supplement an already hardy meal. She is a handsome woman with salt-and-pepper-colored hair as tightly coiled as she is. When her husband springs for a second stuffed potato, she snatches it off his plate.

"You can't have that, Father," she tells him matter-of-factly. "You have high cholesterol." In Hutterite culture, minding your husband's health, weight, and wardrobe is seen as an act of love but, after forty years of marriage, Peter Vetter has learned to circumvent his wife's good intentions.

"Sometimes when she looks away, I pop a chocolate bar in my mouth," he says, stroking his coarse red beard.

"Oh, I know that!" Edna Basel jumps in. "I wasn't born yesterday. Your *Bauch* [belly] tells me everything I need to know and then some!"

Their daughter-in-law, Linda, arrives with a plate of blueberry jam busters and presses her mother-in-law to sit down for dessert. Three cups of coffee and two sweet buns later, Edna Basel's stern exterior has dissolved. "Thank God my husband can read faster than some ministers cause we always finish a bit early," she says, candidly referring to the hefty reading requirements of the baptismal and communion services taken from centuries-old sermons written by their forefathers. Most Palm Sunday services last up to three hours or more, especially if a colony has an elderly minister. "It's a long time to sit on your behind, even if you have a nice big one!" she adds.

Adult baptism is the cornerstone of the Hutterite faith—a voluntary, spiritual commitment with vows that were written hundreds of years ago by early leaders in Moravia. In sixteenth-century Europe, adult baptism was a criminal offense, and mercenaries combed villages looking for suspects, bursting into people's homes, confiscating property, and abducting young children so they could be baptized and placed in Catholic homes. Thousands of believers were tortured and murdered, and most

Anabaptist leaders, including Jacob Hutter, were publicly burned at the stake.

This year, South End Colony has three female baptismal candidates, ranging in age from ninteen to twenty-three. Young adults have to be at least nineteen years old to be baptized, and each applicant must make a formal request of the colony minister. The *Prediger* meets with his council, and if there are complaints against the candidate, the applicant is called in for questioning. If the charges are legitimate, the applicant is given a year to mend his or her ways. Baptismal candidates are required to memorize a great deal of catechism in the High German language and recite them in church on consecutive Sundays prior to being baptized.

On Palm Sunday, the *Teiflingen* (baptismal candidates) will be called to the front of the church where they kneel in a row. The assistant minister pours water into the *Prediger*'s hands, which are cupped in turn over each of the candidates' heads. When the water is released, candidates are baptized and become full members of the Hutterite church and will be served their first communion.

Hutterites quite possibly make the best communion bread in the world. Unlike the flat, unleavened crackers served at many communion services in North America, *Obentmohlbrut* (communion bread) is decadent. Edna uses the colony bun dough recipe, enriches it with cream, beaten egg whites, and extra sugar. The result is a large, light loaf that tastes as creamy as a custard.

The night before the communion service, Edna bakes two large loaves of bread and leaves them in the bakery. The next morning the crusts are removed, and the bread is taken to the church by her husband. It's Edna's job to prepare the communion table with a special white linen cloth used only for this occasion. The wine steward sets the communion table with a gallon of Concord grape wine which is served from four white crockery jugs. The bread and wine symbolize the body and blood of Christ, but they also represent the Hutterite way of life. Just as it takes many grains to make a loaf and many grapes to make a cluster, it takes many members to create a Christian community.

The *Prediger* and the assistant minister tear pieces from each loaf and drink from the jug before handing them down the aisle to the rest of the congregation. They then drink from the two wine jugs before passing them along the rows until everyone has been served. "The men take a good gulp," Edna says, "but the women only take small sips, and there is always some left over." After church, communion is given to the sick or elderly members in their homes, and the leftover bread and wine are brought to the community dining room to be served with the noon meal. "We just polish it all off," says the minister's wife.

Because the Hutterite communion and baptismal services are strictly for baptized members of the community, it excludes most of the colony teenagers, who are left to care for the younger children. The lengthy services provide a window of opportunity for a little mischief, since the head cook and her weekly assistants must also be in church. The community kitchen is the favorite gathering place for these young people who relish being unsupervised.

"Two years ago, the teenagers got into the wine, and when we got out of church we had a bunch of little drunkards running around the colony!" says an indignant Edna. "Well they all got the strap, but now we give them choices. The cook lets them have something from her pantry and freezers. The girls like to make chocolate fudge, but the boys want steak. We don't mind them having a little fun, just as long as it's good fun," she contends. Easter-egg hunts are not part of the culture, but the colony boss supplies each family with store-bought Easter treats. On Easter morning, the head cook boils eggs with blue and yellow food coloring and serves them to the kindergarten and eating school children. "That's the only time of the year we don't have to coax them to eat their eggs at breakfast," Edna says, grinning.

Dating

I am at Velvet Acres Colony, and we are sitting in a large circle of chairs outside the home of Albert and Eunice Hofer. A majestic weeping willow with long, sweeping branches lazily fans us in the summer heat. "Spill the beans, Jolene!" says fourteen-year-old brother Benjamin, prodding his sister when romance comes up for discussion. "I need some advice for getting girls."

Hutterite teenagers often begin dating at age fifteen when they ascend to adulthood and eat in the adult dining room. Weddings and funerals are key opportunities for them to socialize but so are work exchanges, when colonies need help with building barns, slaughtering chickens, or berry picking. Jolene snagged the love of her life helping a relative with a home improvement project.

Last winter, Jolene's favorite aunt from a colony in British Columbia asked her to come to help paint her house. Other families were also renovating and relatives from far and wide had been invited to lend a hand. In the evenings, all the young people met up at the colony machine shop to socialize.

"When Darius introduced himself and sat down next to me, I didn't think anything of it," Jolene shrugged. "He's five years younger than I am, so I brushed him off."

Darius is coming to meet Jolene's parents next weekend, and they are anxious to meet their prospective son-in-law as soon as possible.

"How did you meet your wife?" I ask Jolene's father, Albert Vetter.

"Oh, I fell in love with her the minute I saw her," he tells me, "but she rejected me." His brows lift as he raises the index finger of his right hand. "And you know, that hurt me so much, I left the colony for five years. I couldn't see my life without her, so I just took off." More than thirty-seven years later, the pain of that rejection is still fresh in his mind.

His wife, Eunice, is sitting next to him, wearing a wry smile and not saying a word.

"So how did you end up marrying her?" I asked.

"After a while, I'd had my fill of the outside world and decided I wanted to come back to the colony. I wasn't going to ask Eunice out again, that's for sure. I had my eye on another girl at her colony and one evening, I went there for a visit. As I was walking to my girlfriend's house, I heard someone say, 'Where are you going?' It was Eunice standing in her doorway, watching me.

"When I pointed to a house at the end of the row, she smiled sweetly and said, 'Why don't you come in here instead?' She looked so beautiful the way the moonlight shone on her face, and I never looked back," Albert says, still relieved.

Eunice motions for me to follow her into the house to the back bedroom where she opens a drawer and pulls out a cotton handkerchief stitched with red flowers and colorful Gothic script. In exquisite needlepoint, the lettering reads

Albert Hofer,

My love is true,

Sweetheart for you,

Eunice Mandel

Hutterite "sweetheart hankies" are as symbolic as an engagement ring. They were traditionally given to young men before marriage and draped over the groom's lap during the wedding feast. Just as an English bride might keep her wedding dress, Eunice has tucked the keepsake away in her hope chest. The cherished hankie will be passed on to their children as a lasting symbol of their parents' devotion to one another.

"Do you remember my cousin Hank?" Jolene asks when her mother and I return with a tray of Orange Crush and a plate of banana cream pie.

"You mean Hanky-Panky Hank?" I laugh. Everybody knew Hank from Bedford Colony and his reputation as a playboy.

Hank Hofer had the rugged good looks of the Marlboro Man, and his dark eyes flashed whenever he was in the presence of females. He sang and played guitar, and what he lacked in talent, he made up for in charm. The girls swooned and fell for him like dominoes. He broke more hearts in more colonies than Elvis had hits. And he was a real *Schmierkotz* (a cat that rubs up against you), not only lavishing the pretty young ones with compliments, but also sweet-talking the older women in the kitchen.

When he had conquered the Hutterite world, he left for Alberta, where he found a lucrative job in the booming oil patch. His job gave him considerable purchasing power, and he soon had everything he ever thought he wanted: a brand-new Dodge Ram Long Horn Super Cab, a Street Legal 4-wheeler, and a Polaris Snowmobile. After work, Hank hit the bars and dance clubs where his generous temperament attracted the women, all of them eager to be wined, dined, and romanced.

"He finally got married!" Jolene reports the breaking news.

"She looks just like Shania Twain," Benjamin adds gleefully.

Apparently, Hank thought he was having a great time until he went home to the colony for a visit. He realized that girls on the outside were plenty enticing with their formfitting jeans, low-cut dresses, and enhanced attributes, but something was missing. Most girls on the colony had more depth and weren't as absorbed with their appearance. A certain longing set in, but he could shake it as he blew back to Fort McMurray in his bright red Ram, listening at top volume to the song "Save a Horse, Ride a Cowboy" by country duo Big & Rich. Five years later, he had had his fill. English girls were fun in small doses, but not for life.

He returned to the colony, was baptized, and took himself off the market. In short order, Hank found a girl to whom he could commit. Or more precisely, he claimed the gorgeous girl from Fox Haven Colony who had captured his attention since she was a young teenager. On his visits home to see his mother, he always went miles out of his way to swing by Fox Haven so that he might catch a glimpse of Selena. She was ten years younger than Hank but, at nineteen, she had finally come of age.

Like Hank, young Hutterite men eager for a taste of the outside world sometimes leave the colony for a few years, but the greatest lure back home is the love of a good woman. "Marriage is like a leather shoe," said Albert, getting philosophical. "You polish and care for it, and it will last you a lifetime."

"I hope you told that to the tomcat, Albert," Eunice quipped, finishing the last of her Orange Crush.

Later that evening I steal down to the colony playground to watch the young people engage in a lively game of volleyball.

It's been raining and the volleyball court is a mud pit, but that doesn't concern either the guys or the girls. They don't mind getting dirty so long as they win the game.

It takes me back to when my siblings and I first started going to a mainstream school. Our competitive Hutterite nature is about the only thing that served us well in our new life. We went from being shunned to most wanted when it came to team sports.

My older brother Alex, who had an acute stubborn streak, once forced the teacher to let us take on the entire school in a softball game because he resented the disparity with which we were being treated by other students when they didn't need us to help them win their games. There were only six of us to go against the other thirty-five primary school children, but the teacher found it impossible to dissuade my brother from his absurd idea. Exasperated, she caved in, certain the end result would bring him back to his senses. But Alex coached us in playing such a strategic game that we beat the entire school 40–0, earning ourselves a grudging respect and a much-needed boost of self-esteem.

The spirited rivalry that I once witnessed in Fairholme is plainly evident here too. Some of the players are from a neighboring colony and, amid the volleys and serves, there is plenty of teasing and flirting between the sexes.

Two of the young women are wearing blue nail polish on their toes, others have neatly plucked brows, and one girl has blond highlights in her dark brown hair. Though these subtle changes are departures from when I lived on the colony, nowadays they are generally accepted by more liberal Hutterites as a way for teenagers to express individuality.

I can't help noticing that some of the middle-aged women have also started to color their hair. Frequenting a hair salon would be out of the question, but an in-home job to ward off going gray is obviously becoming an option. Earlier, when we were alone, I noticed Eunice's roots were showing, and I asked her if women her age have started to use hair color, something that would have been unthinkable in my mother's era. Back then, the most popular means of self-expression was eye wear. I remember my mother having some pretty spectacular cat-eye glasses that even had small rhinestones on them. Glasses remain very popular with Hutterite women. Even those who don't need them are known to have a pair.

"We're not supposed to, but we do," she said honestly. "Our men don't even notice," she adds, suppressing a laugh by putting a hand over her mouth. "Besides, it's none of their business!"

Halfway through the volleyball game, I am joined on the sidelines by two teenage girls. They are from another colony five miles west of Velvet Acres. Their long skirts and shoes are covered with mud, and they are breathless from exertion.

"Did you come to Velvet Acres to flirt with the boys?" I tease.

"You bet!" says the pretty blond one.

Her name is Nolene, and her dark-haired friend is Joanna. Both of them are nineteen years old.

"So who's the cutest guy in the game?" I prod.

"Kevin," they announce, pointing to a strapping broad-shouldered male spiking the ball.

"But he's my first cousin, so I can't have him," says Nolene, pretending to pout. "We're not allowed to marry first cousins. It's against colony rules."

"How convenient for me," clowns Joanna, rubbing her hands together.

For the past 200 years, Hutterite young people have chosen marriage partners of their own free will with relatively few restrictions. But prior to that and going back to our very beginnings, couples were matched at twice-yearly matching ceremonies. Male and female members of the various *Bruderhof* communities in Moravia were required to inform the elders if they wished to be married. The elders would bring all those who had made their intentions known together, once in spring and once in fall, placing males and females on opposite sides of the room. The males would be given a choice of one of three women. If the woman that a man chose agreed to be his wife, the pair would be married that same day. But if she turned her suitor down, she would have to wait until the next matching and the disheartened male would be offered a second selection.

In addition to work exchanges and opportunities offered when communities are located relatively close to each other, most young men on Hutterite colonies earn the use of a vehicle every four to six weeks to visit girls at colonies of their choice. As soon as a young man is given a seat in the adult dining room, he is included in these ventures. The arrival of a pickup full of eligible young men is met with the kind of enthusiasm one would expect from any given colony with young women.

"It's very exciting, especially for our fifteen-year-old girls who finally get to join in," Joanna tells me.

"We don't really pair up at first. We get to know each other before we start dating. It's fun to just hang out and socialize. That

*The potato caucus
leaving the kitchen*

Children in school desks

*Young men shoveling snow off roofs.
No one is paid a wage.*

*Upon marriage, colony members
receive bound copies of the Hutterite
Chronicle, the Holy Bible, and
songbooks in Gothic High German*

Jam busters

Children at play

Because of their beauty and workmanship,
sweetheart hankies are sought after by antique dealers

*Though divorce is not an option, Hutterites
generally have happy marriages*

*The love of a good woman brings many
runaway boys back home*

Women making big cheek pockets for soup

way you get to know everybody and then you figure out who you like best," she says, brushing clumps of mud from her skirt.

During the day, the young males are folded into the colony work cycle and toil alongside their male counterparts in the fields and barns. They are assigned beds in the homes of various community members and take their meals in the colony kitchen. By the same token, the young women they came to see are expected to do their own work during the day. It's only in the evenings when everyone gathers to have fun.

Joanna and Nolene tell me the favorite hangout in most colonies is the machine shop because it's spacious and gives them much-sought-after privacy where they can enjoy a round of beer, play guitar, sing, and play some pool or ping-pong. The colony provides everyone of legal age with one case of beer per month, so the boys usually bring some from their own stash while the head cook makes meat slices, cheese, and bread available to the young women so they can make sandwich platters to take to the shop.

"If the boys don't behave or if they drink too much and become disorderly, we hear about it and we discipline them by canceling the next outing and making them wait an additional six weeks to get a vehicle," one elder informs me.

"What about the girls?" I ask Nolene and Joanna. "Don't you get any trips?"

"We get trips to the lake to go swimming and have a BBQ. And we also get trips to town. The boys use their travel opportunities to chase us but we use ours to go shopping," laughs Nolene.

"What do you shop for?"

"I'd rather have new shoes than almost anything else," she exclaims. "I love Keen shoes, but I also really like the Mary Jane style. Our colony gives us one new pair a year, but I have to buy myself an extra two pairs a year. I have to have three new pairs of shoes a year to be happy," she insists.

"How do you earn enough money for two extra pairs of shoes?"

"Our colony gives us twenty dollars a month. It's not much, but its more than others get. If you save, it can add up quite quickly, especially since so much of our personal items and clothing are provided by the community. We're also allowed to clean English people's houses in town, but only if there is no colony work. And sometimes we make and sell pies on our own time and keep the money."

Restrictions for earning your own money vary considerably from colony to colony. The margins that Nolene and Joanna enjoy could be considered quite liberal.

"And what do you love?" I ask Joanna, turning to her.

"I love fabric," she gushes. "We get four new dresses from the colony every year. We get to choose the fabric from a selection that the head seamstress provides for us. She gets her material from Mook Fabrics, and when the samples arrive, it is so exciting, we can hardly breathe. The older women choose the darker fabrics, but we get to choose lighter material as long as there is not too much white in it. The older women prefer crepe, but the younger girls like us prefer cotton. I buy fabric for two extra dresses," she beams.

"Are you allowed to have cell phones?" I ask after spying Nolene texting.

"Yes!" she says hastily.

"No, we're not!" Joanna jumps in.

"OK, we're not supposed to have computers or cell phones, so we are secretive about it," Nolene clarifies. "Our older people are dead set against us having them because there is so much bad stuff on the Internet, and it's so easy to become distracted from life or work by our cell phones. But the fact is we live in a computer age, and they can be useful. It's almost impossible not to have some sort of attachment to these things when they are all around."

"We try to be respectful of our elders, but we can't just do everything they want us to do," adds Joanna. "We work hard and we need to have some fun. It's just that we have to be sneaky about it," she winces.

"Joanna, Nolene, get in here!" shouts one of the boys throwing the volleyball at us.

"Those boys can't win a single game without us," Joanna remarks as she and Nolene run back into the mud pit.

Die Hulba (The Engagement)

It's raining autumn leaves when I pull into Lewis Colony in western Saskatchewan. The evening sky is Prussian blue, and the air smells faintly of clean laundry. The lights in the community kitchen cast a warm glow, and through a row of windows I can see a blur of pleated skirts moving from place to place.

I have been invited to Celia and Jerry's *Hulba*, a Hutterite engagement celebration that takes place a week before the wedding. It is customary for the bride to move to the groom's colony, and the *Hulba* is an elaborate send-off for the bride-to-be who will formally say good-bye to the community that she has lived in all her life.

Celia is twenty-four years old, with eyes that dance behind designer eyewear and porcelain skin free of makeup or jewelry. Like most Hutterite brides, Celia has sewn her own engagement and wedding dresses, along with all the bed linens that she will need in her new home.

Celia's fiancé, Jerry, is a handsome twenty-six-year-old who has already grown the neat beard required of all men when they marry. The pair met for the first time when he came to Lewis Colony two years ago to show the men how to operate their new computer in the hog barn. His colony had one just like it, and he helped them iron out the glitches while acquiring a girlfriend in the bargain.

"She caught him; he didn't catch her," Celia's mother later tells me. "He is too shy and too slow."

The head cook is pulling large roasting pans with stuffed ducks out of the Rational oven. The sixty birds are browned and crisped to perfection, and the sight of their mahogany, salted skins gives me the urge to dive in for a taste test.

The colony women and visiting helpers are tossing, testing, and tasting Celia's *Hulba* feast. "Please don't take my picture," shouts Dorothy Basel, one of the senior women, as I step into the kitchen, camera in hand. Because photographs are considered graven images and posing for the camera has always been forbidden, taking pictures must be done with discretion. Many older members have never had their photo taken but are often the most photogenic.

"You're supposed to say hello before you scold me," I tell her. She puts down her pot of gravy and welcomes me with a warm hug.

"I've come to see your new shoes," I whisper in her ear. When someone on the colony gets married, all the women receive a new pair of shoes from the community. Up goes her ankle-length skirt so I can have a good look at her top-of-the-line leather Birkenstocks. Built for comfort, they may not be stilettos with four-inch heels, but the thrill is identical.

She points me to the menu just inside the door: Roast Duck, Crab-Stuffed Pasta Shells, Mashed Potatoes with Gravy, Crunchy Vegetable Bake, Strawberry Asparagus Salad, and Fruit Pizza for dessert. It's making me hungry!

The community dining room was prepared for the celebration by the young women. The decor is simple: red roses and baby's breath have been placed in sealer jars for centerpieces and drinking glasses are tucked with soft blue, pink, and white napkins. Decades ago, decorating for a wedding was considered too worldly, but mainstream ideas are gradually seeping into the culture. A long head table anchors the far end of the dining room for the bride and groom, their families, and the head ministers. A decal on the wall behind the head table bears a passage from the book of Ruth in the Bible: *For where you go, I will go and wherever you stay, I will stay. Your people will be my people, and your God will be my God.*

Extra tables have been added to accommodate visitors, including friends and family from other colonies as well as associates from the outside world. The extra guests have tripled the size of the colony of ninety-one members.

"They're coming!" shouts one of the young girls peeking out of the kitchen window. The *Hulba* ceremony has ended and men and women are spilling out of the church. Celia and Jerry have just made informal vows of commitment, a custom that takes place at the bride's colony a week before the wedding and carries the same weight as wedding vows. An integral part of *Hulba* celebrations, it is called *Zomstelln* (the putting together).

When the kitchen doors burst open, I am swept into the current of community members and guests flooding the dining room. Heads nod approval when they see the decked-out tables. As men and women slide the length of the benches to their places, I am squeezed in with the women just as applause breaks out and the bridal couple enters hand in hand. *Hulba* dresses are typically green or violet, but Celia looks stunning in a gold brocade dress. "We worried it would be too flashy," Celia's mother tells me, "so we checked with the other women and even with Jerry's mother, and everyone approved." The younger women are in awe as Celia sparkles toward the head table on the arm of her groom.

Among the first to know of Jerry's intention to marry Celia was the minister at his colony. A prospective couple must be baptized and in good standing in the community. *Prediger* Michael Hofer called a meeting of his advisors (the front bench) to discuss any issues or complaints against Jerry that would deem him unfit for marriage. When he received their support, he drew up the traditional letter of request in High German, which was delivered to the *Prediger* of Celia's colony.

> *Dear Prediger Elias, Lewis Hutterite Colony,*
>
> *The peace of God and the love of Jesus Christ be with you. We hope that you are in good health both physically and spiritually. We are coming to you with a request. One of the Brothers from our community has asked to marry a Sister from your community. We hope that you will by the grace of God be supportive.*
>
> *We want your help to arrange a wedding to which you are all invited.*
>
> *Thank you in advance for your assistance.*
>
> *Kindest regards from us all*
> *Prediger Michael Hofer*
> *Prairie Ridge Colony*

The prospective groom, his father, and two of his uncles undertook the 600-kilometer journey to Celia's colony to deliver the letter by hand. It is considered bad luck for women to accompany them, so Jerry's mother and sisters stayed behind.

Satisfied that the request came with *Prediger* Michael's blessing, *Prediger* Elias also gave his conditional blessing to the groom and sent the party to Celia's parents. Arranged marriages are not part of Hutterite culture, but receiving your parents' consent is a vital part of the process and remains a valued Hutterite tradition.

These days, most brides and grooms are well acquainted with their prospective in-laws, but that wasn't always the case when telephone service and transportation was not as sophisticated. If the girl's parents didn't approve of the match, they could influence their daughter not to accept the proposal and the dejected suitor was sent away, or a process of negotiation would begin.

At the *Hulba*, the head minister recites a brief table prayer before a dozen young men pour into the dining room with trays containing pop, glasses of wine, and cans of cold beer. *Hulba* and wedding feasts are always served by the colony men, a role reversal that they perform with such cheer and ease that it's hard to believe that weddings are their sole kitchen experience. They lower the loaded trays to the center of the table and offer guests a drink of their choice. Minutes later, they float down the aisles teasing and being teased, their trays stacked with the salad, entrées, and dessert.

I help myself to the crab-filled pasta shells. Rich and delicate, they are the perfect foil for the vinaigrette in the strawberry and asparagus salad. The ducks are served whole so diners can whittle off the cuts of their choice. I chew on a crisp piece of breast skin, and my head bobs up and down with pleasure. The woman across from me dives straight for the dessert and hands it to her neighbor, who follows suit.

The talk at our table turns to an etiquette lesson for new brides, who have the challenge of fitting in with a whole new peer group and routine at their husband's colony. Each community has its own quirks and preferred methods of work. Sometimes a new bride will find herself at a colony that is not as prosperous as the one in which she was raised. Personality clashes and different styles of doing things can make the adjustment difficult.

"She should keep her mout shut for a whole year," the Hutterite woman on my right opines, shaking her drumstick at the woman across the table. "Even if you're right, don't go into dere kitchen and say dis is how we do it at our colony. But after a year, you've earned da right to an opinion, and you can say what you want."

The guests are still eating when a cluster of young women with songbooks line up in front of the children's table, obscuring their view. Unwilling to take their eyes off the bride and groom, half a dozen young girls peek out from behind the singers' skirts to watch the couple exchange loving glances and whisper in each other's ear at the head table. After the wedding, such public displays of affection would not be suitable. Even to see a couple seated together in the dining room is novel, for after the marriage Jerry will return to eating with the men and Celia will be seated across the aisle with the women.

As the meal comes to a close, the cook and her helpers wear satisfied smiles as they lean against the door frame of the entrance to the dining room. Pans of leftover dessert pizza in a cream cheese and crumb crust are being divided and taken to individual homes. I am presented with a pie too. It's not every wedding where a guest leaves with a dozen fresh buns and a dessert pizza!

After the customary prayer of thanks recited by the colony minister, the bridal couple leaves for Celia's house to prepare *Geschenken* (to receive blessings). The rest of the community follows. Duck carcasses and platters of leftover food are snatched up and brought into the kitchen where a clutch of twenty women, including English visitors, stand in a circle around a communal sink, washing, rinsing, and drying the dishes with bath towels. Within half an hour, the food has been put away, the tables are wiped, the floors are washed, dishes are returned to the cupboards, sinks are cleaned, and the lights are out.

Mike and Susie Wollman have invited me to their living room where we wait for Celia and Jerry, who walk from home to home with a flask of whiskey and some shot glasses to offer a toast and accept a blessing from all members of the colony. It is also an occasion for the bride to say her formal farewell to her home community.

"Celia is strong willed but Jerry has a good way of handling her," Susie tells us. "If a husband is very opinionated he needs a strong woman to stand up to him. If he is soft hearted he doesn't need a sledgehammer for a wife. If he's a big talker you have to have a woman who loves to listen, like me"—she rolls her eyes— "or you invite someone over who has big ears and a small mouth."

We all jump to our feet when the radiant couple enters Mike and Susie's cozy home. Celia is holding a tray of glasses, and Jerry pours the whiskey.

Mike Wollman holds his glass aloft, an impish grin on his face. "May your wife be as crazy about you as mine is about me after all dese years," he toasts, before downing his Jack Daniel's and returning his glass to the tray.

When the laughter dies down, his wife fires back, "And may you be a better liar den my husband after all dese years."

After additional blessings for a long life, a loving marriage, and two sets of triplets, the bridal party disappears into the night.

Tomorrow morning, Jerry will take his betrothed home to Prairie Ridge Colony, 600 kilometers northwest of Lewis Colony, where a home has been prepared for them. Traditionally, the engaged couple arrives at the new colony by five o'clock on Saturday afternoon, on the heels of a truck filled with the bride's belongings. When Celia was baptized, her gifts from the community included bedding, draperies, and forty pounds of goose feathers for making duvets and pillows. She also received a king-sized bed, two bedside tables, an armoire, a dresser, and a top-of-the-line sewing machine, a serger, and a cutting table.

Jerry had to wait until he married to receive his share of gifts from the community, including his allotment of feathers, and a new king-sized bedroom suite for the bridal home. The couple is given a fridge, a kitchen table and chairs, rocking chairs and sofas for the living room, and money to buy dishes, cutlery, and other small household items.

The entire community will gather outside the colony kitchen to welcome Jerry and Celia, and children bearing large bunches of balloons might run out to the road and flank the bridal vehicle as it slowly makes its way onto the colony. At the end of the regular nine-thirty Sunday morning church service, Celia and Jerry will make their formal vows of marriage. There are no wedding rings: Celia will wear a traditional Hutterite blue wedding dress, and Jerry a new black suit and white shirt, made by his mother. The couple will stand in front of *Prediger* Michael, clasp hands, and make their vows. Jerry will pledge that he will not disgrace his wife by getting into trouble with the law, and should he suffer shipwreck of faith, he will not take her or their children off the colony. Celia will be asked if she believes his intentions are sincere and whether she desires to accept him in good faith without complaints.

A special dinner is served after the church service. There is no honeymoon, but the couple will have Monday off to put their freshly painted home in order.

Jerry will be given a permanent position, such as field boss, cow man, or German teacher and will become a voting member of the community. In the days ahead, when Celia's adjustment to her new community poses inevitable challenges, her husband will be expected to defend and protect her. Those early years of marriage cement a strong and lasting bond, and although divorce is not an option, most Hutterites do in fact have happy and fulfilling relationships.

It's midnight before I take my leave from Jerry and Celia's *Hulba*. I'm escorted to my car by animated teenage girls. When I opine that women receive more substantial gifts from the colony than their male counterparts—more fabric, more toiletries, more shoes—they readily agree. "That's cause when the boys marry us, they get *everything*!" they chime.

- -

HUTTERITE WEDDING CAKE

30 boxes Duncan Hines White Cake mix
5½ cups butter
15½ cups lard
27 cups icing sugar
1 cup vanilla
5 cups Cool Whip

Make 30 boxes of Duncan Hines White Cake mix and bake according to instructions.

Cream butter and lard on high speed until white and fluffy. Gradually fold in icing sugar, vanilla, and Cool Whip. Ice cakes when cooled.

CHRISTMAS DAY NOON MEAL MENU
Roast duck
Spring rolls with hot pepper sauce
Shrimp with garlic butter
Steamed beans in mushroom sauce
Vanilla ice cream with chocolate sauce and nut toppings
One glass of chokecherry wine per adult

THANKSGIVING DAY SUPPER MENU
Deep-fried turkey
Bread stuffing
Garlic potatoes
Steamed carrots and cauliflower
Corn
Fresh buns
Pumpkin cheesecake
One can of beer per adult

EASTER SUPPER MENU

Quartered lamb braised in sauce
Baked potatoes
Stuffed mushrooms
Crab rolls with sweet sauce
Cabbage salad
Dilly bar ice cream
One vodka and cranberry drink per adult

Leah's Diary

Monday, August 31

I'm frazzled today because fifty ministers are coming here for a meeting, and that puts a lot of extra strain on me. The women are all wondering what's on the ministers' agenda, but I'm concerning myself with what's on my menu. We'll find out soon enough about the ministers because our men are not that good at keeping secrets.

If a minister has a situation in his colony that he can't handle, he will call other ministers together to ask for advice. Usually it's a disciplinary matter.

Last year, a *Buah* [unmarried young man] requested to get baptized, but his minister said, *No way, he hasn't listened to a thing I've said all year.* At the meeting, the other ministers told him, *You're right. If he can't be respectful and take instruction, he is not ready for baptism or marriage.*

We all expected that young buck to be mad and run away from the colony, but we heard later that he smartened himself up, and he is getting baptized this year.

The ministers will all be arriving for supper tonight. Of course, I want to make something that they will enjoy. We're having beer can chicken, boiled new potatoes, green beans, sliced tomatoes and cucumbers, and 300 cobs of corn. Our dining room is not large enough to seat everyone at once, so we'll eat in two shifts. I told my husband to round up some of the men to help serve the ministers, because I won't be able to handle all that myself.

All the *Predigers* will be staying with colony members, so I'll send a platter of cold cuts, two bags of buns, and some bananas home with the women.

For breakfast tomorrow, we'll need 25 pounds of finger ham, 5 fillers of eggs, toast, and raspberry jam.

The noon meal tomorrow is fried chicken (200 pounds), fries (140 pounds), gravy (triple the recipe), romaine salad (triple the recipe), and ice cream for dessert. We'll also serve coffee and water.

For *Lunche*, I've asked the women to make Rocky Mountain Chocolate Chip Cake (triple the recipe) and Rice Krispies Squares (triple the recipe), and we'll put together fresh fruit plates.

For supper, we'll need three blue tubs of mashed potatoes, 300 breaded lamb chops, carrots, parsnips, and coleslaw. We've had a terrific garden this year so there's lots of vegetables to choose from. I've decided to serve butter tarts for dessert. I've asked the cooks on bake week to triple the recipe.

Wednesday, September 2

All the black hats have gone home, and everybody said
we did a great job. We are having a simple supper tonight:
macaroni and cheese, sausages, and a green salad. We love
our homemade sausage and, in the fall, I put it on the menu
three times a week. The men get 4½ inches of sausage each;
the women get 3½ and the children are given 3 inches.
If a family has four male adults, three female adults, and
two children, they will get a sausage ration of 34½ inches
at mealtime.

Some women want me to separate their family's
sausage before serving. Some want me to leave their sausage
allotment whole (altogether), because their husbands or
older sons will want more than their 4½ inches and the
young ones can't eat their full portion.

Everyone takes leftover sausage home or freezes it for
snacks. I always serve my leftover portions on days when we
have fresh buns because they go together so well.

Notes on Wedding for Mark and Janice

Jeannie and Elsie baked 2½ pails of buns.

Cathy and Margaret cooked.

SATURDAY

8:45 a.m.   Women made sandwiches, 32 loaves of bread, ham,
and hard cheese

Made fruit basket, cheese and pepperoni plates, and
evening lunch plates

Supper   Beef stew, mashed potatoes, corn, crab salad with cukes and tomatoes around the edge, Jell-O and whipped cream in glass for dessert

SUNDAY
Wedding   Cooked 50 old hens for noodle soup (25 Saturday
Dinner   morning and 25 Saturday evening). Turned skillet to 150 degrees and baked 30 fryers in oven. Had potatoes, vegetable plate and dip, fresh buns, sauerkraut, pickles, pistachio pudding for dessert, beer, wine, and pop

Baking for family prepared and sent to the house 8:00 p.m. Had hot dogs (160) and salad with wedding cake. After evening lunch, all women washed the floors with mop

ࢣ RECIPES

Christmas

Usten

six

Prune Money

"The person who wants to know everything doesn't live very long."

Hutterite women love to shop for fabric

"I CAN MAKE ANYTHING but babies," Helena Stahl tells me as she guides me through her spacious sewing room in the basement of her home. The gifted head seamstress at Little Mountain Colony has been married for eighteen years but is childless.

The sewing room is clean and bright with polished wooden floors, large windows, and a stream of sunlight flowing through the open curtains. It's clear that her talents extend beyond sewing dresses and shirts to making baby blankets and feather duvets, quilting, knitting, needlepoint, and hooking traditional Hutterite rugs.

Hutterite women sew clothes for their entire family: a *Pfaht* (cropped white blouse), a *Mieder* (vest), a *Kittel* (ankle-length, gathered skirt), a *Fittig* (pleated apron), and a *Wannick* (jacket) for the women, and black pants, jackets, and shirts for the men. Children's clothes are identical to the adults, except girls under the age of six wear bonnets instead of polka-dotted headscarves. Women at Little Mountain get two new dresses a year, seven new blouses, and six new aprons.

"Our fabrics come from Marshall Fabrics in Lethbridge, Mook Fabrics in Medicine Hat, and Mitchell Fabrics in Winnipeg," says Helena. Samples of material are left in the community kitchen every January so the women can select patterns of their choice. "Our dresses used to be very bright with lots of flowers, but some of the men complained that we drew too much attention to ourselves. Now our fabrics are more modest, and our rule is that the design on the material should not be bigger than a cow's eye." Young children are the exception, and mothers love to dress them in brightly colored or flowered dresses and shirts.

Helena selects black cloth for pants and jackets for all the men and boys, along with material for the men's shirts. She also chooses material for the women's aprons and blouses. Aprons have to be a different color than the dresses, at least at this *Lehrerleut* community. Years ago, a head seamstress would make semi-annual buying trips to the city to purchase material for the entire community, including fabric for wedding and *Hulba* dresses. Now, many young brides are given the money to purchase fabric of their choice.

Each family also gets five yards of bedding per person per year, including babies. Most sheets, pillowcases, bed skirts, and duvet covers are handmade, but items such as shoes are store bought.

Decades ago, the shoemaker was responsible for making leather shoes for everyone on the colony. He still supplies some of the men's work boots and repairs shoes, but has diversified by fixing horse saddles and harnesses, sharpening kitchen knives, and crafting fine leather flyswatters.

Women receive one hundred dollars annually to buy a pair of shoes. The latest footwear craze for the younger women at Little Mountain is Alegria and Dansko, but they also love Clarks and Skechers. Additional monies are also given to the women to purchase bras and feminine hygiene products.

Every June, each man gets three new pairs of suspenders, eight pairs of boxer shorts, and six pairs of socks. The men write their sizes and color preferences on a piece of paper and give it to the colony boss, who makes the purchases on his next buying trip. Everyone also gets a supply of toothpaste, soap, and body wash, and the women are always gifted with an extra treat of special lotion. All other personal needs fall under the purview of the colony boss, whose medicine cupboard is stashed with an assortment of vitamins, Advil and Tylenol, NeoCitran, Pepto-Bismol, Vicks VapoRub, Polysporin, Wonder Oil, hydrogen peroxide, and Metamucil.

"The women get something new for the home every year," Helena tells me. "It might be a new set of blinds or a coffeepot. Every ten to fifteen years, we get a new sofa set, but for major purchase years, the women only get one new dress instead of two."

Women take four weeks' vacation a year to visit their home colony or a favorite sister or friend. Ideal vacation times are in spring and winter when the community workloads are lighter and the yearly fabric allotments have been parceled out. The downtime is often spent sewing or crafting with mothers and siblings.

"Why don't you try it on," Helena urges when she sees me admiring the stitching on one of her dresses. Because my family left Fairholme when I was ten years old, I never had the opportunity to learn to sew traditional Hutterite clothing, an important part of the ascension to womanhood. Helena watches me as I slip into her cropped white shirt. Over that comes a vest and then the matching jacket, which closes with snaps down the front.

I step into the dark, pleated skirt and smile when I see the safety pin that is hitched to the band. It allows a women to make a clever little adjustment should she gain or lose a bit of weight. I tuck my *Jackey* into my skirt before adding the final piece, an apron, whose long strings I wind twice around my waist and tie in the front so as not to obstruct the carefully crafted pleats that flow down my backside. Beautiful pleats are big deal around here—the litmus test of how well one can sew.

In my grandmother's era, I would also have worn a ridge, commonly referred to as the *Wurscht* (the sausage). Two inches in diameter, the sponge coil was tied around the waist and fit beneath the skirt like a bustle to keep the fabric from clinging to the body. This produced an element of surprise for any number of men on their wedding night, including my grandfather, who looked at his disrobed new wife in utter astonishment and exclaimed, "*Is es yo nichs mir ebber!* There is nothing left of you!"

"Let me do your hair," says the seamstress, pointing me to a nearby chair.

She rakes my long bangs over my face, and I feel the sharpness of the comb as Helena creates a part down the center. "I want to look as good as you and the other women in my *Tiechel*," I tell her, wondering how she's going to get the kind of height required to make my head scarf sit as well as hers. The slow, sweeping motions with which her brush sweeps over my scalp feels so luxurious it gives me goose bumps. Helena's ten-year-old niece keeps peeking around the corner watching us, and I am reminded how as a young girl growing up in Fairholme Colony, my best friend, Catherine, and I often loitered behind doors to eavesdrop on the older girls' conversations, which inevitably were about boys, new dresses, and sometimes about a glamorous English woman named Elizabeth Taylor. We listened wide-eyed to accounts of her beauty, her jewels, and her scandalous love affairs. The only time we were allowed into the rooms where the women were lounging was if we offered to brush their hair. It was down to their waists, thick and lush, and we would stand behind them on the sofa and leisurely move the brush from the top of their heads all the way down their backs. It kept them happy and us in the know, and that was all the compensation we ever needed.

Helena clasps the hair on the left side of my part in both hands and starts to *Drah* twist it as tightly as she can from the top of my forehead to my ear. After fastening it with a hairpin, she repeats the sequence on the other side. Because my hair is too short to sweep up into a bun, Helena puts it in three separate ponytails, which she pins together at the back. Hutterite women twist their full length of hair right to the waist before pinning it into a bun. The hairstyle was popular in Europe in the sixteenth century, and most Hutterite women still prefer this same neat, modest style. To give the the desired lift, Helena places what looks like a kitchen scouring pad on my crown and secures it with a dozen hairpins. I hear a snap as she shakes out the *Tiechel* and centers it on my head. She brings my face toward her and folds the sides of the fabric against my cheeks, tying a snug knot under my chin. "*Hetz bist du schean.* Now you're beautiful," she proclaims, happy with her work. I jump to my feet and head to the bathroom, where the only mirror in the house hangs above the sink. My mother stares back at me. Wow, I look just like her. And that ingenious scouring pad gives me the sought-after lift in the back of my head that women the world over strive for.

Helena tells me that when they first arrived in North America in 1874, the women used to dip their *Tiechel* into a basin of milk and press them with the weight of a hot iron to give them the desired stiffness. After a few days of wear, the headscarves took on the odor of sour milk and required constant washing, so the women switched to a mixture of flour and water.

Starching used to be compulsory, and headscarves were so stiff that you could stand them on the night table and they wouldn't collapse. The younger generation began to grumble that their *Tiecheln* were uncomfortable and that starching was unnecessary. The practice was abandoned decades ago by the *Schmiedelent*, but only recently by the other sects. Although decisions like this are voted on by men on the colony, the women serve as a powerful lobby group and, if persistent, will eventually get their way.

Hutterite women on the colony are no different than women in the outside world. They are just as interested in trying the latest brand of shampoo or adding to their feminine mystique with bath powder and body lotions. Earning private money is against the rules, but colony members receive between ten to twenty dollars a month allowance from the community to spend as they wish. It's much less than they need for coveted items like extra fabric or a leather purse, so many of the women generate extra pocket money by selling chokecherries or saskatoons, homemade feather quilts and pillows, baby blankets, and innovative products like sliders— hand-crocheted floor pads worn under a boot to stop the men from tracking mud on a freshly washed floor.

This unauthorized revenue is sometimes referred to as *Schwischem Gelt* (prune money). The phrase was coined fifty years ago when Tabitha Basel from Stone Wall Colony confronted the boss about the paltry one-dollar-a-month allowance that the women on her colony were given back then.

"What could you possibly want money for?" the boss demanded. "You have everything you need."

"I need money for prunes," Tabitha Basel said curtly, implying that she suffered from constipation.

What she really wanted was an extra fifty cents to buy perfume at the local drugstore. When the colony boss finally gave in to her appeal, she was miraculously relieved of her ailment and became the proud owner of a bottle of Evening in Paris.

Helena's father, George Vetter, steps in the door as we head upstairs for coffee. He is a soft-spoken man with hair as unruly as Albert Einstein's.

"What do you spend your monthly allowance on, George Vetter?" I ask, curious about the male spending habits.

"Oh, I buy anything that doesn't work. I love fixing things. I take my ten dollars to the secondhand shop first chance I get, and I buy broken electrical appliances like toasters and waffle irons. I fix them and give them to whoever needs one. We live near the reserve, and we give to our Indian friends too."

Helena shakes her head and passes her dad the coffee cream. "That's why his nickname is Tinker George. Since he retired as chicken man, he's been busier than ever."

There is a lull in the conversation when George Vetter's gray eyes soften.

"The last time I received my allowance, I was in Walmart waiting for my ride. I saw a most beautiful card and when I opened it, I saw it had a love note written inside. This is how I feel about my wife, I thought to myself, but I have never bought her a card before. I decided to buy it and wrote *Love, George* on the bottom of the card. I sealed it in the envelope and slipped it into the book on her night table.

"Before we go to bed my wife and I read together," he continued. "That night as I settled into my side of the bed, I kept one eye on her because I wanted to see her reaction.

"I could see how surprised she seemed as she slowly tore the envelope and read the card. She just froze for a while and didn't say anything. Finally, she turned to me and said, 'George.' There were tears in her eyes.

"The next day when she started phoning our daughters to tell them about the card, I couldn't help overhearing. She sounded so excited. But in the afternoon, Helena and her sisters all came over to the house looking worried and serious.

"'Is something wrong with you, Dad?' they asked me. They thought I was saying good-bye to Mother. They thought I was gonna die," he wails, running his hands through his white bouffant.

Frietich, auf die Kneah (On Your Knees Friday)

I can hear them all the way from the community kitchen at Birch Creek Colony, their voices rising and falling in rich harmony as I walk toward the open doors of the slaughterhouse, which the women are cleaning.

They are singing "River Road," an old Crystal Gayle hit, and I fall in with them.

"Go stick your nose in," head cook Darlene Gross told me as she filled my arms with variety boxes of Revel, Creamsicle, and Fudgsicle ice-cream treats.

I have been in the colony bakery all morning helping make Poppy Seed *Krapflen* Pockets for the women doing the cleaning. I hadn't tasted them for so long that my heartbeat quickened as I rolled out each silky square of pastry dough, stuffing it with a composite of inky poppy seeds, fresh cream, raisins, bread crumbs, sugar, vanilla, and cinnamon. The limbs of a Hutterite kitchen reach to all corners of the community, and hard work is rewarded with special indulgences, whether it's for the men combining the fields, stock hands branding cattle, or the women cleaning the slaughterhouse.

Elma and Ashley, the women on bake weeks, teased me for being too methodical and sentimental in the way I fill each *Krapfel* to the max, carefully crimping the edges, imagining what they're going to taste like, and wondering out loud if they will live up to the sweet, gritty poppy-seed pockets I loved so much as a child in my own colony. The two will bring the baking as it comes out of the oven, along with coffee and cold drinks, but the head cook sends me over in advance with the ice cream.

She is the barometer of the community workforce and concerns herself with timelines. It's an unseemly hot day. The sun is beating down on me, drawn like a magnetic field to my dark Hutterite clothing, and I am dissolving as fast as my armload of ice cream. Cool damp air greets me as I enter the slaughterhouse as do arcs of arms and a swag of skirts. Close to twenty women between

Colony shoemaker

A Hutterite woman Drahs *(twists)
her hair*

*Picture of me wearing the
traditional Hutterite Tiechel*

*Young girls are gradually transitioned
from braids to* Drahnen *(hair twisting)*

*Sliders, an ingenious way of
keeping the floors clean*

Young girl washing porch

*Women washing floors to
a high shine*

Maria Basel and baby

*Older people are valued for their wisdom
and storytelling*

the ages of fifteen and fifty-five move like a symphony, each with her own bucket of hot water, rubber apron, gloves, and a stash of homemade rhubarb sterilizer and *Speck Saften* (lard soap). Young girls are high on scaffolds washing walls and the ceiling, while the older ladies sweep great swaths of soap on stainless steel tubs, tables, and lower walls. Their wash strokes keep time with their singing, and they all move to the same measured, rhythmic beat.

Cleaning is the quiet obsession of Hutterite women. It's in their blood, a rich part of their heritage. In their early beginnings in Europe, Hutterites were leaders in sanitation and hygiene. Hutterite bishop Peter Walpot developed stringent guidelines for hand washing and standards of cleanliness that were so advanced and effective that Hutterites routinely escaped the epidemics that spread through Europe in the mid-1500s, killing thousands of people. Regular washing of hands was mandatory on all the *Bruderhofs*, and in colony schools, children with infectious diseases were isolated and laundry was sterilized.

Centuries later the fixed weekly cycle of cleaning at Birch Creek echos the same high standards of cleanliness set by their ancestors.

Every spring and fall, when the harvest is done and the dust has settled in the nearby fields, Birch Creek is awash in buckets of soapy water. Every building gets a thorough cleansing. The walls, ceilings, windows, and fixtures of the kitchen, schools, barns, shops, and individual homes are scrubbed top to bottom.

The colony's weekly cleaning schedule is as important as its weekly menu and is posted by the head cook where everyone can see it. The community kitchen and dining room are cleaned after every meal until they gleam: dishes are gathered, washed, and put away; tables are wiped; and floors are mopped. Ceiling fans and vents are washed weekly, and so are the walls, shelving, drawers, and benches. Even the grout between the floor tiles in the kitchen is scrubbed with soapy water and toothbrushes every cycle. On Mondays and Thursdays, the colony laundry room with its ten top-of-the-line washing machines and dryers are hosed down and the floors and walls scrubbed. Once a month, the colony's entire cache of dinnerware, cutlery, and serving dishes is taken out of the cupboards and washed with bleach to guard against viruses.

Walpot associated cleanliness with healthful living at a time when those principles were not generally accepted. Only decades later did French chemist Louis Pasteur explain how germs were spread, leading to the establishment of sterilization methods for the nineteenth century. Walpot considered good hygiene a spiritual requirement spawning the Hutterite motto *Rheinlichkeit geht mit Seligkeit*—cleanliness is an attribute of godliness.

Colony cleaning hits the high bar with *Freitich, auf die Kneah* (On Your Knees Friday). Mops are put away, and all floors in the kitchen, the dining room, the church, the schools, and the women's homes are hand washed. Chairs and benches are placed upside down on tables, and the women get on their knees and wash every square inch.

My mother has permanent dents in her knees from the years she spent washing floors at the Hutterite colonies where she grew up. After we left the colony, we discovered in more ways than this that the colony never left us. Every Friday at midnight in our lonely little farmhouse, you could find Mother on her knees in the kitchen, all the dining room chairs turned upside down on our table, washing the floor by hand. The serenity of the night, the clean smell of the soap, and the sheen of her tired linoleum floor was a ritual she found pleasure in.

Twice a year after the collective cleaning is complete, the women invite their relatives from other colonies to come and help with clean their homes, and they in turn go to their relatives' colonies to return the favor. Floors, walls, ceilings, cupboards, and even furnaces will all be washed down, bedding sanitized, mattresses shampooed, and the curtains laundered. Children under five are given to the care of grandparents or relatives so the work is not interrupted. This is also the time when young daughters are apprenticed. My mother's older sisters used to come from Deerboine Colony to clean our house, wash walls, strip beds, and paint closets. I loved being included in small tasks such as washing their coffee cups or sweeping up after them.

These yearly cleaning frenzies provided the women a chance to air out more than their houses; it was an avenue to air their grievances. I would bring them steaming cups of *Kreitertee* tea, a herbal blend also referred to as *Kreichtertee* (complaining tea) while they talked about difficult husbands, nosy colony neighbors, or the dull fabric choices made that year by the head seamstress. The sisters found solace in each other's company, and I loved the engaging way they talked and laughed about their dilemmas. I am feeling devious as I spill the ice-cream bars on a nearby table, grab a clean rag, and jump into a cooling tub being purged with a cloud of comet by Hannah-and-a-Half. That's what everybody calls her because she has more personality than is considered appropriate for just one person.

Oven Cleaner

2 cups water
1 tablespoon cornstarch
2 tablespoons vinegar
3 tablespoons lye
2 tablespoons ammonia

Mix together water and cornstarch and bring to a boil until thick. Add remaining ingredients. Cool. Use rubber gloves to protect hands and apply to oven with a brush. Let paste sit for hours or overnight. Wipe clean with a wet cloth. Rinse with clean, hot water. Clean racks separately in same manner.

Hannah-and-a-Half is constantly being chided by the other women for "saying things she should only think and asking questions she has no business knowing the answers to." But they are quick to acknowledge her overriding redeeming quality: she shares what she knows with the rest of them.

"Yo, the only time she comes around is to help us eat ice cream!" Hannah-and-a-Half shouts to everyone within a five-mile radius, nearly knocking the younger women off their scaffolding. She puts me in a neck hold and rubs some Comet on my nose, and I return the favor. By the time we call a truce and heave ourselves out of the drum, we have an amused audience and streaks of white all over our dresses.

"You're better at making us laugh than helping us clean," one of the women points out. My deficiencies withstand plenty of razzing like this.

The poppy seed *Krapflen* arrive with carafes of coffee and a tray of cold drinks, and the women descend the scaffolds for a break. We consume the wildly delicious poppy seed pastries. Our teeth are besieged with deposits of tiny black seeds, and we look not unlike a bunch of pirates with very bad teeth!

Kronka Kechin (Special Cook)

I am holding baby Emily, inhaling her sweet, milky fragrance. She is one month old and no bigger than a minute: bald, wrinkled, and utterly perfect.

Her mother, Lydia, beams with pride from across the room. She looks so much like Raphael's *La velata* that I can't help staring. She has the same round face, dark hair, large, brown eyes, and understated noble bearing as the subject of the painting by the Italian Renaissance master.

Maria Basel is Lydia's mother-in-law, and when she heard that I was at Little Mountain, she called and told the head cook, "Send her over here."

The next morning, I arrived at Big Gate Colony, fifty kilometers south of Little Mountain. Maria Basel is the *Kronka Kechin*, a special cook who looks after the dietary needs of the elderly, the sick, and new mothers like Lydia.

The cook has a deeply dimpled chin and elbows. Standing over the soup vat in the kitchen, she stirs and tastes, inhaling and adding to her vessel. Instead of fried food or heavy meat dishes, Maria Basel prepares special soups daily, like *Nuckela* or *Gritz Soupen*.

"Soups are easy to digest and give you energy," she tells me. Plump cuts of chicken, *Totsch*, steamed vegetables, homemade yogurt, and waffles in a splash of whiskey are other favorite menu items.

That evening, Maria Basel's living room is filled with her extended family, including her two elderly sisters. Emma and Bara are in corner rocking chairs with melon-sized balls of yarn on their laps, their knarled hands deftly slipping wool over and under the knitting needles.

The women are both in their eighties. Cherished for their wisdom and humor, they are the oral storytellers, as entertaining as Lucille Ball or Jerry Seinfeld. Encouraged by half a dozen teenagers sitting on the floor around them, Emma embarks on a story that underscores the very practical nature of Hutterites.

"Yo, when we were young mudders, Bara and I had our cook weeks together," she begins, her needles furiously gobbling up yards of blue wool. "We were serving canned chicken for da noon meal, and one of da jars we opened didn't smell quite right. But dose were da dirdy turdies and da colony was struggling, so we didn't feel right about trowing it out. We didn't know what to do because every time we stuck our snouts in da jar, we got a little whiff of someting not quite right. And do you know what Bara said to me? She said, 'Emma, you only have two children. You taste it.'" The room erupts and Bara unapologetically rushes to her own defense. "Dat's right! I had five children by den and I tot if she got poisoned, better two children widout a mudder dan five."

"How many children do *you* have?" inquires Maria Basel, peering at me over her smudged spectacles.

"I only have one," I reply.

"You're a poor producer," quips the senior member of the knitting club, a sly smile on her face. "You weren't even half trying!" her sister chimes in. She's been enjoying some Cheezies, and her small mouth has a bright orange ring around it.

"That's all God gave me," I tell her, looking down at Emily, fast asleep in my arms, her little chest rising and falling with each breath.

In previous generations it was not uncommon for women to have fourteen to sixteen children, but most existing families are half that size. Children are a great source of joy and pride to Hutterites, and new mothers have an extensive support system.

As soon as her daughter was born, Lydia entered *Die Wuchen*, an eight-week period of special treatment extended to women after the birth of each child. In addition to being exempt from colony duty, new mothers chose an *Abwärterin* (one who waits on you), usually their own mothers or an older sister brought in from another colony to be their personal caregiver for the first six weeks of the baby's life. New mothers also chose a *Lukelah* (a baby holder) from all the young girls on the colony between the ages of eleven and fourteen. The position is coveted, and parents often petition on behalf of their adolescent daughters to influence a mother's choice. The role of a *Lukelah* is to help care for the infant, as well as clean the house and look after the other siblings. The position generally lasts one year or until the mother gives birth to a new baby and selects another apprentice.

The gift package from the community for a woman's first child is extensive. Lydia was given her choice of crib, high chair, playpen, stroller, and car seat. Fabric to make five new maternity dresses was supplied by the colony seamstress, along with forty yards of material for diapers, bonnets, and dresses for Emily. Baby powder, creams, lotions, and twenty pounds of feathers for baby pillows and quilts were delivered before Lydia arrived home from the hospital.

So too is a bushel of *Rascha Zwieboch* (roasted buns). Delightfully crunchy, these biscotti-like biscuits are the perfect dipping companion for tea, coffee, hot chocolate, and soup.

New mothers also receive ten pounds of sugar, a jar of fresh honey, a large tin of coffee, and packages of raisins and prunes. Two cases of beer and a forty-ounce bottle of whiskey are also gifted to the family so visitors can come and toast the new arrival. Abstainers are offered an equal share of non-alcoholic beverages such as pop or juice.

At eight weeks, Lydia will return to work gradually, doing small jobs such as washing dishes and peeling potatoes in the community kitchen. At ten weeks, she will start to ease into her regular routine, and by sixteen weeks, she will return to regular cooking and baking rotations with the rest of the women, although she will be given generous blocks of time to breast-feed and check in on her daughter.

Lydia's thirteen-year-old *Lukelah*, Carlene, attentively refills my teacup and protectively peers over at the bundle in my arms. She is taking her apprenticeship seriously and no doubt wishes I would grow tired of her little charge so that she could have a chance to hold her.

Emily is fussing and wants to be fed. Carlene scoops her up and takes her to Lydia who is flanked by a four-year-old boy and a five-year-old girl. They are the children of her twenty-eight-year-old sister who died two years ago of cancer only three weeks after being diagnosed. Now they belong to her. Lydia stepped in to look after the children, and she brought so much strength and stability to the devastated family that they couldn't imagine life without her. She married her widowed brother-in-law a year later. Emily is their first child together and has brought renewed joy, not only to this little family but to the entire community.

The 1929 Ordinances List of Items to Be Given to Mothers at the Birth of Each Child

¼ pound of tea
3 pounds sugar
1½ pounds coffee
1 cup flannel leaves
9 boiled eggs
2 bushels *Rascha Zwieboch*
4 ounces cinnamon sticks
1 cup of cream or ice cream daily
2 quarts whiskey and 1 quart wine for toasts *

Each child receives eight pounds of feathers at birth, another two pounds at age ten, and an additional two pounds at age fifteen, for a total of twelve pounds.

* During Prohibition, alcohol was replaced with two extra pounds of coffee.

Remedies and Superstitions

I'm waiting to have a visit with Sora Basel at Blue Hills Colony. She is the colony sage, and I want to talk to her about traditional herbs and remedies used by Hutterite people. It's her nap time, so I've invited myself next door where I inadvertently get a primer from a quartet of women relaxing on the front porch.

"If you worship someone for being beautiful, you might cast a spell on them and make them sick," Miranda Decker says as she waters her two pots of purple pansies.

"Oh, Mom, I don't believe that!" says her daughter Tanya from a nearby chair.

"Me neither," agrees her cousin Amy, wrinkling her nose.

"Girls, it's true," Miranda's sister-in-law Carol chimes in. "It's called *Schreien* (bewitching someone), and our older people always told us to be restrained and not look at someone who is very attractive too long or too hard, or something bad can happen to them."

Carol is an arresting woman with luminous green eyes and rich auburn hair.

"I wouldn't believe it if I hadn't experienced it myself," she says ardently, shaking her head.

"When I was a teenager, I went to a wedding at another colony," claims Carol, sipping a glass of iced tea. "I was enjoying my meal when suddenly I became very weak and light-headed. I quickly left the dining room and hurried to my aunt's house to lie down.

"After a few minutes a woman came in and asked me what was wrong, and I told her I didn't know. Something just came over me and I didn't feel well.

"'It's because of me,' the woman confessed. 'I was admiring you so much I cast a spell on you.'

"She lifted my eyelids and licked out each of my eyes and spit into a cloth. I immediately started to feel better. So much better I was able to return to the dining room and enjoy the rest of the wedding."

"Why did she do *thaaat*?" Miranda recoils.

"I don't know. She told me that's what she had to do to break the spell," Carol says, fishing in her pocket for a hankie.

"I have made a lot of people sick," I confess, surreptitiously taking inventory of all the people I've looked at too long or admired too much over the course of my lifetime.

"Me too!" Tanya and Amy declare in unison.

As we share a laugh, I hear my name being called.

"Sora Basel is up," a young girl shouts from her grandmother's house. "Come over."

When I get there, my subject is running around the house with her little oxygen tank looking for her glasses. "I don't know why I can't *shnaufe* [breathe] today," she complains.

"You're not plugged in, Mudder," her husband, Esau, scolds, jumping to his feet. He checks the outlet and, sure enough, Sora Basel has unplugged herself again.

She has a heart condition that requires her to be on supplemental oxygen. Her cord is so long it travels throughout the house and doubles back whenever she does.

"Be careful you don't trip or hang yourself," Esau Vetter warns as I step over a maze of cords.

"*Ach ya*," Sora Basel sighs as she plugs in the kettle.

Sora Basel and Esau Vetter are both in their nineties. They live next door to their son and his family. Their descendants number fourteen children, seventy grandchildren, twenty-three great-grandchildren, and two great-great-grandchildren. Teenagers trail in and out of their spacious home as we visit.

The pair decides to sit opposite me at the dining room table because, as Esau Vetter puts it, "I can't hear and my wife has 'cadillacs' [cataracts]."

"*Voter* [father], I can see as good as you can," she differs.

The vulnerability of advanced age has made their lived-in faces as beautiful as a child's—hers pale and round as a full moon, and his angular and deeply tanned, except his forehead, which is in startling contrast to the rest of his facade because of his habit of always wearing a hat when he goes outside.

Between them, they possess generations of valuable data. Sora Basel used to be the colony's midwife and was prominent among her people for her practical cures and advice for people's ailments. "Goose fat," Sora Basel says with certainty when I ask her about the most important remedy in her arsenal. "*Warum*? Why?" she asks rhetorically.

"Because goose fat reduces inflammation and dat is da most important ting. Inflammation is very bad for da body," she says, tapping a jar of goose fat on her varnished dining room table.

"When da children had a chest infection or da croup, we just rubbed a little goose fat on der chests and back and covered da area wit a warm *fitz* [cloth], and it was wonderful," she says, her voice raspy. "It works just as good for grown-ups."

"Goose fat is also good for *Reisen* [arthritis], isn't it, *Voter*," she continues, looking at her husband.

"Well, it's purdy good, I have to say," replies Esau Vetter, rubbing his right knee.

Sora Basel jumps up when the kettle starts to whistle.

"*Sitz nieder, Mueter*. Sit down, Mother," says a voice from the kitchenette. Her daughter-in-law Wilma has slipped in the door with a cake, and we carry on while she serves us *Lunche*.

When I ask Sora Basel about Carol's bewitching story, she nods. "We picked up superstitions like dat when we lived in Russia," she admits, rearranging herself on her chair.

Wilma serves us hot cups of chamomile tea and squares of carrot cake crowned with an inch of cream-cheese icing. My piece is twice the size of the ones she gives her in-laws.

"I dare you not to finish it," Wilma chuckles, bending over me.

"Here, put some honey in your tea," Esau Vetter insists, handing me a glass jar of clover honey produced at the colony bee house.

Hutterites are honey lovers, having extolled its virtues for centuries. Jars of honey can be seen lining tables in community dining rooms as well as in individual homes. In Fairholme, our honey jars never left the tables except to be refilled. Salt, pepper, and honey were the three must-have condiments. The perfect companion to fresh bread, honey was also used by the adults to sweeten their coffee.

Many colonies have apiaries and produce honey for the healthful antibiotic properties that this ancient superfood is known for. As children, we ate it by the spoonful, especially in the evenings when it was served in our *Kreitertee*, into which we dunked crunchy crusts of *Rascha Zwieboch*.

My paternal grandfather was the bee man at Fairholme Colony, and I was both terrified and fascinated by his line of work.

The bee house was up a little hill behind our house on the colony. I could see it in the distance from my back bedroom window.

Oltvetter (Grandpa) was a gruff character with vivid blue eyes. His entanglements with people made him regard his bees ever more affectionately.

When the mood struck, I would go with him. My craving for a piece of honeycomb dripping with liquid candy only marginally outweighed my terror of being stung.

I never went really close, preferring to watch from a distance. The first thing Grandpa would do was go to a hive that had a lot of activity and stretch out his arms so the worker bees would sting him. He told everyone who would listen how beneficial it was for arthritis, and when I tell Sora Basel about this, she says their old beekeeper did the same thing.

"*Dos vet ach Russisch sein*. It's probably another trend we picked up from Russia," she contends.

When my grandpa was sufficiently stung, he put on his protective clothing and went to work.

Mother claims my visits came to an end when I was about five years old. She was at home sewing when she heard bloodcurdling screams that echoed throughout the colony. Looking out the back window, she saw me running toward home, my grandfather stumbling after me in his beekeeper's veil and overalls. He was shouting for me to stop, but I was heading straight for home and the safety of my mother.

I was panicked that I had a bee in my ear. Mother tried to calm me so she could have a look, but I continued screaming and flailing until my grandfather arrived.

He grabbed me away from her and hit me on the top of my head with such zeal it momentarily knocked me out. But he also killed the bee. It had lodged beneath my *Mütz* bonnet and was tangled in my hair, and my grandfather instinctively knew that's where it was.

"*Gut gemeint, aber schlecht gemacht, Maria.* I meant well, but I overdid it, Mary," he is said to have told my mother as she picked my limp body off the floor.

My affection for honey survived my grandfather's blow, and I accept Esau Vetter's advice and add a spoonful of honey to both my and Sora Basel's cup of tea.

We bite into our pieces of carrot cake and nod our approval to a grinning Wilma who is standing over us. It is divine. The moist, coarse slab is brimming with walnuts, pineapple, and finely grated carrots, the perfect justification for a thick summit of cream-cheese icing.

"Our ancestors were some of da best doctors in Europe," Esau Vetter says, wiping a crumb from his ducktail beard as we resume the conversation. "But dey killed dem all off and burnt our medicine books."

In sixteenth-century Moravia, Hutterite doctors were in great demand. Known as barber-surgeons because they cut hair as well as performed surgery, they traveled widely, carrying with them wagonloads of compounds and ointments to treat not only the people in their *Bruderhof* communities but commoners and kings in the regions. They were highly skilled for their time, schooled in the art of pharmacy, and proficient in practices such as blood cupping, believed to mobilize blood flow and promote healing. Leaders in hygiene, barber-surgeons were famous for their therapeutic bathhouses administered by professional *Bader* (caretakers of the baths). It irked Catholic leaders that the bathhouses' most loyal clients were noblemen and Catholics themselves, who were said to throng to them on Saturday nights.

The three most notable Hutterite physicians of that era were Georg Zobel who was credited with saving the life of the emperor at the imperial court of Rudolph II in Prague; Conrad Blossy who was recognized for his work in extinguishing a 1612 epidemic breakout in Zurich, Switzerland; and Balthasar

Gollar, the personal physician of the imperial ambassador Count Herberstein and of Cardinal Dietrichstein who hated Anabaptists with such passion he eventually expelled them from Moravia. The persecution that followed was so severe it led to the near annihilation of the Hutterite people. Gollar was killed, his pharmacy destroyed, and so were the medicine manuals and formulas he used.

Upon their arrival in North America, Hutterites began to frequent mainstream doctors but community members who had a certain knack or therapeutic aptitude remained the first line of defense.

"When I was a young boy, our chicken man was also da colony dentist," says Esau Vetter, licking the last bit of icing from his thumb. "He pulled everybody's teet and even did fillings," he discloses. "He was a bit rough, but he did a good job. Even our English neighbors came to him. He charged dem twenty-five cents for every toot he pulled out and fifty cents for a filling."

"How did he get his materials?"

"Dey said he was good friends wit da dentist in town who showed him a few tricks, and so he went and ordered some supplies from a catalogue and set up a little shop in da chicken house. Pretty near put da town dentist outta business!" he chuckles.

When my father was a young boy, he broke his leg after falling off a horse, and it was the colony bonesetter who reset it. Similarly, midwives like Sora Basel were relied on to deliver hundreds of babies in their time. My own mother gave birth to two of my brothers with the help of the colony's midwife.

"I delivered most of da over-sixties on dis colony." Her eyes brighten.

"But we lost some, too," she says softly. "And den you have to help da poor mudder overcome it. I sent for udder mudders who lost a baby because dey knew how it feels and could do da best job of *traisten* (consoling).

"*Goose Speck, Rheinlichkeit, undt Kreitertee.* Goose fat, good hygiene, and herbal teas were mostly what we used," Sora Basel says, holding up four fingers instead of three.

"*Undt Selichkeit.* And living a godly life," Esau Vetter jumps in, accounting for the fourth finger.

"*Yo dos is es bista, Voter.* Yes, that is even more important, Father," she agrees.

"We just went in da bush like da Indians and picked flowers and herbs to make tea. Alfalfa was good for morning sickness, wild peppermint cleaned da body, and flannel leaves we gave to all da new mudders. A cup of flannel leaves was always part of da gift from da colony so dey could make tea. Flannel tea helped dem relax and git a good night's sleep so dere breast milk could come in properly," Sora Basel explains.

"But we also grew our own teas," she says, adjusting her glasses. "Chamomile and poppy tea were bote good. In da evening, we made a very mild tea for cranky and colicky babies from poppies.

"We didn't know dey were used for drugs until da RCMP told us," Sora Basel tells me soberly.

"Dats because you and Dora Basel got busted," Esau Vetter scolds.

"Well, we were in da poppy patch to check on da plants, and dese two men come along and asked if dey could have some poppies. We didn't tink not-ting of it. We just cut off a few plants and gave dem some. Da next day da RCMP got after us. Oh, dey were mad! Dey told us dose guys were big drug dealers in town. We nearly fell over," Sora Basel says, her nostrils flaring as she raises both her hands in surrender.

"Da RCMP wouldn't let us grow poppies for five years just for dat," Esau Vetter grumbles.

"Dat was a hard lesson," Sora Basel nods.

My own mother told me when she was a teenager her colony of Old Rosedale grew poppies mostly for seeds, which they used for baking, but they also made tea from the leaves and gave it to fussy or colicky babies. She said they figured out the danger when one of the mothers made her baby's tea too strong and the baby didn't wake up for two days.

I receive a pat on my back from Wilma for polishing off my extra-large piece of cake as she moves in to refill our teacups.

"We still grow poppies for their seeds every three years," she says, clearing the table of our empty plates. "But we are monitored by the government, and we aren't allowed to make tea or anything else with them anymore. We just harvest the pods by hand and, after we give them time to dry, we peel them open and extract the black seeds to make *Krapflen* (poppy seed pockets), pies, and cakes."

"*Speck Saften* [homemade lard soap] is da best for *Reinlichkeit* [cleanliness]," says Sora Basel, coming to her third point. "It's good for washing dishes, floors, clothes, and people. All da colonies still make it."

"The *Klanaschuel Ankelen* and the over-sixties always make the soap," says Wilma, herself in her mid-sixties. "If Mom didn't have to wear oxygen, she'd still be making it too."

"I sure would," Sora Basel agrees.

"We usually make soap in the fall. The younger women clean the colony, and the older women make the soap. We get up at four o'clock in the morning and we work till eleven at night. We make it in a cauldron behind the slaughterhouse that is as big as this table," she says, launching into the finer points of the operation.

"We start by putting bones at the bottom of the cauldron. Cow, pig, lamb, chicken, you name it," says Wilma. "Just as bones add flavor to your soup, they also add strength to soap. Bones give soap its sharpness. So does pig skin, which we also add for potency. The lye will eventually dissolve the bones and the skin.

"We combine the lard we've rendered over the year from butchering: pork, beef, goose, lambs, and ducks. To 600 pounds of lard, we add 36 five-gallon pails of water. We liquidize the lye with cold water before adding it to help prevent it from splashing.

"Look," she says, showing me little lye dots on her forearm. "You have to be very careful with lye," she warns. "When I first starting making soap, I got splashed but didn't realize it until it got really itchy. Now we wear long gloves and smudge our faces with vinegar because it creates a protective barrier and neutralizes the lye," Wilma explains.

"You let the lard and lye cook for two and a half to three hours. But it has to be boiling. You can't begin timing it until it starts to boil. You'll see when the soap starts to separate from the liquid. It gets really creamy. To get the soap to rise to the top, we add half a gallon of salt. Once the soap is ready to be put into molds, the younger women help us.

Speck Saften · Homemade Lard Soap

600 pounds lard
36 5-gallon pails water
150 pounds lye
½ gallon salt

Put the entire lard and all pails of water into kettle. Dissolve lye in cold water and add. Boil 2½ hours, making sure it boils evenly all over. Turn off heat and add ½ gallon salt and 2 pails cold water to let settle. Let stand 15 minutes before removing from the kettle.

"We don't allow the children anywhere near us because the lye is dangerous," Wilma says seriously.

I remember lazy August days in Fairholme when the colony women were making *Speck Saften* in a cove behind the community kitchen. We were kept at bay with threats from the senior women who were stirring the bubbling cauldron wielding long paddles. But the danger drew us like flies, and we circled them like a pack of wolves, watching as billows of smoke rose up from the vessel and the soap makers withdrew their faces and squinted as they stirred.

"We let them set in the molds for three to four hours before we cut them into bars," says Wilma. "They should by rights cure for three to four years so they're nice and hard, but we often use ours before they cure entirely because we have very hard water at our colony and we need lots of soap."

I am reminded of the attic in the community kitchen at Fairholme where hundreds of crudely cut bars of soap stood in crates, curing. My childhood friend Catherine and I loved to go up the stairs on hot summer days because the heat gave the soap a pungent scent that we both loved.

In my mother's era, the women would put a bar of soap into the washing machine with the clothing and take it out during the rinse cycle, but on colonies today they have liquefiers and pulverizers for the *Speck Saften* they use in the washhouses.

"Last year," Wilma says with amusement, "we were just about done when it became so windy I said to the women, there is only one solution to this. The kindergarten children have some Halloween masks, and we will have to put them on for protection. Well, we were laughing so hard, all of us with those stupid masks on, that we nearly fell into the cauldron ourselves."

"What was your mask?" I ask, curious.

"I was the president of the United States," she states matter-of-factly.

Imagining Wilma as Barack Obama gives Eli Vetter and me the giggles. Sora Basel disappears into a back room and returns pressing a bar of gold bullion into my hand.

"*Doh, nemm.* Here, take it," she says.

It's a bar of *Speck Saften*.

I inhale its fresh scent. "It smells like my young years," I tell her.

The spring day has dissolved into long shadows as we say good-bye on the front porch.

"What do you tell women who have difficulty conceiving?" I ask Sora Basel.

Her face dissolves into a smile.

"Hang a diaper on da wash line and just leave it dare," she replies, a hint of mischief in her eyes.

- -

WILMA'S CARROT CAKE

2 cups granulated sugar
1⅓ cups vegetable oil
3 extra-large eggs, at room
   temperature
1 teaspoon pure vanilla extract
2½ cups plus 1 tablespoon
   all-purpose flour, divided

2 teaspoons ground cinnamon
2 teaspoons baking soda
1½ teaspoons salt
4 cups grated carrots
1 can crushed pineapple, with juice
1 cup raisins
1 cup chopped walnuts

Beat the sugar, oil, and eggs together in the bowl of an electric mixer until light yellow. Add the vanilla. In another bowl, sift together 2½ cups flour, the cinnamon, baking soda, and salt.

Add the dry ingredients to the wet ingredients. Fold in the carrots and pineapple. Toss the raisins and walnuts with 1 tablespoon flour. Add to the batter and mix well. Pour into buttered 9- × 13-inch pan.

Bake for 55–60 minutes at 350°F or until a toothpick comes out clean. Allow cake to cool completely before icing.

For the Icing:

Two 8-ounce packages cream cheese
½ pound butter, at room
   temperature

1 teaspoon pure vanilla extract
1½–2 cups icing sugar

Mix the cream cheese, butter, and vanilla in the bowl of an electric mixer until combined. Add the sugar and mix until smooth.

Leah's Diary

Thursday, January 8
5:30 a.m.

It's going to be a hectic morning in the kitchen. We always have pancakes with syrup for breakfast on Thursday. Some colonies will have a piece of bologna or fried eggs along with that, but, for some reason, people here want a slice of cheese. I get out the cheese and batter, and by 6:30 I am ready to start frying the first batch of pancakes. I'm also breading the beefsteaks that we will have for dinner. The assistant cooks are forever cleaning something, so they're alternating between dishes and getting things ready for peeling potatoes. The women peel spuds Mondays and Thursdays. The assistant cooks must get their thinking caps set on straight when all the women are there to do the work. Otherwise, those two would be left with a lot of potatoes to peel for even one missed meal. Usually they have lots of help remembering, because everybody can see what is needed on the weekly menu that I hang in the kitchen every Friday afternoon.

10:30 a.m.

I'm in the kitchen to fry beefsteaks. We all love our steaks, especially the men, and I don't want to overcook them. I put the first batch on the skillet and, as they sizzle away, I measure out noodles for soup, since we always have fresh noodle soup with this meal. The last batch of steaks is just about done, and I take them off the hot surface as the dinner bell rings.

1:30 p.m.

Tomorrow is bun-baking day. The women on bake week
will measure or weigh out the dry ingredients, but it is my
job to determine the amounts of buns or bread we will need
in a week. If we need hamburger or hot dog buns, these will
also be made along with the Friday buns. I have my menu
planned for next week, and on Monday for dinner we will
have pork roast sandwiches, so today I have to take the
roast out of the walk-in freezer so it thaws by Sunday. I also
take out the twenty packages of bacon and forty pounds of
hamburger meat for next week and stick it into the chiller.
It is all so routine; after a year of being head cook, you just
remember which jobs go with which day. But I went through
a lot of sticky notes my first year just so I would remember
everything. Mind you, there are still times I will forget
something, but then I tell myself that nobody's perfect.

3:00 p.m.

We are having spaghetti and meatballs for supper, so I have
to be in the kitchen early. We use twenty pounds of raw
hamburger for the meatballs, which I season while the oil is
heating in the skillet. Usually one of my sisters-in-law will
come and help me shape them with small ice cream scoops.
That way, they are uniform in size. I weigh the spaghetti so
the assistant cooks can boil the pasta when they get here.
We usually simmer four gallons of our own tomato juice
and add a gallon of water and spices for our homemade
sauce. This makes a lot of spaghetti, but the meal is a
favorite of everybody here.

Lots of our members like something sweet after the meal, so we usually have canned fruit, Jell-O, or pudding. Any rich desserts like cakes and pies are sent home to be eaten for *Lunche* or when the family gathers. Today we're having canned crabapples after the spaghetti. It's the assistants' job to get fruit from the basement and open it, but it's my job to see that each person gets their share.

5:00 p.m.

My assistant cooks have caught up with the mountain of dishes from making supper. It's time to ring the bell for the mothers who have children less than six years of age. The cooks and I can have our meal now. Both ministers had to go to the city on business, so it's not so rushed today because we won't be having church. There is always something for me to do here, so I will just keep on working until supper instead of going home to wash up. Sometimes, when I'm at home, I will walk over to the kitchen to do something that I forgot earlier, and then I have to give myself a shake and go back home to do something for my family instead. Being the head cook definitely takes some getting used to.

6:00 p.m.

It's time for supper now, and I'm starting to panic that there won't be enough meatballs. It all depends how many people will eat at home. If there are fifteen or twenty people in the city, food is taken home for them by a family member. We

always need more food if we have lots of separate dishes
to fill and, yes, it is a common thing for the head cook
to panic. I'm usually right when I worry, because even if
there is enough for the adults, we usually run short when
feeding the six- to fourteen-year-old children who eat after
the adults.

⁂

7:00 p.m.

Everybody has been fed, and if the kids did not have
enough, I'll be sure to hear the complaints from my own
children first. I might as well go home and face the music. If
I ever run short, I usually end up heating leftovers from the
day before, but the children are not too happy about that.
It's been a long day, so maybe I'll brew myself a fresh cup of
coffee and put my feet up for a while.

⁂

Friday, January 9
6:00 a.m.

It's quiet in the kitchen when I get there this morning. The
women on bake week have been here since 3:30 a.m. mixing
buns. Yesterday, my assistants boiled twenty-four quarts of
milk so the women could mix the buns bright and early this
morning. Now, they're scrubbing the stainless steel pots and
pans to a nice shiny finish so everything is spotless when
their cook week is done. At 5:30 a.m., the women aged
seventeen to forty-five come over to punch down the dough

and roll the buns. They are all done in twenty-five minutes, and they all rush back home to catch a few more winks or find quiet things to do until the rest of the family awakens.

When they go home, I start my day. I put the breading on the pork chops and put them back in the fridge until closer to the noon meal. This morning, we are having eggs and sausage for breakfast with bread and a variety of jams and honey. I slice the sausage and set it out to be steamed a few minutes before breakfast.

Today is Friday so everybody, including me, washes their floors and thoroughly cleans their homes for the weekend. I don't get mine done in one shot like most of the women because I must constantly go to the kitchen.

I can smell the buns baking in the ovens. We always have fresh, warm buns for coffee break at 8:30 on Friday mornings when we clean our homes. Mmm.

10:30 a.m.

I'm back in the kitchen making the pork chops for the noon meal. The last ones will be ready just in time for the dinner bell. The gravy is hot, the potatoes are roasted, and the veggies are steamed.

They are wolfing down my meal with not a compliment but nobody is complaining either, so I have to be satisfied with that. The ladies stay after dinner on Fridays to wash the dining room floor. During the week, we wash it with mops, but on Friday it's done by hand. While they cleaning, I am free to go home and relax a bit.

1:30 p.m.

I've had a nap and will finish washing and waxing my
bedroom and bathroom floors. The kids have to stay out
of their rooms until the linoleum dries. I'm trying to hurry
so this cleaning spree comes to an end before the day is
over. We're having fries and chicken cutlets for supper, but I
don't need to go to the kitchen right away since the week is
winding down.

3:00 p.m.

Everybody has gone back to work. I usually bring out my
recipe books and food list to make a menu for the next
week. All head cooks know the walk-in freezer by heart. If
I'm running short of a certain meat, I will tell the boss, and
he sees to it that some will be butchered, which is always
done in large quantities. The men will butcher pigs and
cows, but the women come and cut it up in pieces for beef
stew. The boss usually cuts the steaks and the roasts. We
don't waste, so he weighs the meat and packs it in exactly
the amount that is needed for a meal. Of course, I'll tell him
if I run short so that he will add a few pounds next time.

4:00 p.m.

I'm already starting to prepare for next week. If I have
any poultry to cut into nuggets, strips, or cutlets, I will do
this now. The chicken cutlets for supper only need to be
warmed, so I'll post the menu while I wait for first call.

5:15 p.m.

The cooks have had supper, and I can ready myself for church. Tonight is hair-washing night for my two daughters. With their long, thick hair, this takes just about all evening.

I hang the menu in the kitchen every Friday afternoon. My assistant cooks choose the salads and vegetable dishes for each meal. After supper, all the women crowd around it to see what we are having next week and to discuss which meals they are most looking forward to.

Saturday, January 10
6:00 a.m.

It's a cold morning, but it's cozy in the kitchen. It smells like fresh coffee and *Speck Saften*. The assistant cooks are on their hands and knees washing the floor in the cooking areas. They clean under all the appliances and behind everything that can be moved. I try not to walk over their washed area. Today we are having cheese—cheddar for some, processed slices for others—it depends on what they prefer. The cook has to either have a very good memory or a page in her reminder book of what everybody wants. I slice up the cheese, and the assistant cooks will put out the bread later. Sometimes, there will be leftover sliced ham or sausage to finish, so I will set them out too. Today I have to rush because we are having little donut droppings for dinner, which I mix and the assistants help to cut. Then we fry them in hot oil until they puff up. We call them *Strudelen*, and anybody can take some home for the morning coffee break. The rest will be served for dinner with *Saura Soupen (Sour Soup)*.

MENU FOR THE WEEK

MONDAY
Breakfast Cheese and ham
Dinner Vegetable soup, Old Man's chicken stew, canned cherries
Supper Ginger beef, mashed potatoes, raisin and prune *Mues*

TUESDAY
Breakfast Bacon and eggs
Dinner Fried cottage-cheese pockets, beef stew, canned sweet tomatoes
Supper Pizza pretzels, homemade pork sausage, canned peaches

WEDNESDAY
Breakfast Rice Krispies
Dinner *Geschtal* (ragged bits of pasta) soup, stuffed ducks, mashed potatoes and gravy, lime yogurt
Supper Lentil soup, ham sandwiches and fries, canned Bing cherries

THURSDAY
Breakfast Pancakes and cheese
Dinner *Maultoshe* (Big Cheek soup), beefsteaks and scalloped potatoes, fresh yogurt
Supper Spaghetti and meatballs, canned peaches

FRIDAY
Breakfast Eggs and sausage
Dinner *Nukela*, pork chops, boiled potatoes and gravy, raspberry Jell-O
Supper baked beans, bacon, fresh buns, oatmeal cookies

SATURDAY
Breakfast Sliced cheeses, ham, bread, and jam
Dinner Sour soup and *Strudelen*, Saturday *Wurstch*
Supper Lamb rack, roasted potatoes, Stripe-It-Rich dessert

SUNDAY
Breakfast Wieners and fried eggs
Dinner Noodle soup, roasted chicken and rice casserole, chocolate pudding
Supper Tomato soup, beef wraps, baked apple with whipped cream

7:00 a.m.

The *Strudelen* are done, and the bell is ringing for breakfast. I make a dash for the door so I can help my daughter with her hair and make breakfast for my son who is milking. I fry him some eggs and crackling. Everybody has crackling with their coffee break at 8:30 since there is not such a big spread at breakfast. Now I'm free to clean house and to do Saturday chores. The week has to wind down at home, too. Of course, being a mother, I can find something to do right up to the last minute before going to the kitchen.

11:30 a.m.

We always have the noon meal fifteen minutes earlier on Saturday. The cooks have made the *Saura Soupen*, which is ready to be served. For meat, we're having a treat: chicken feet and gizzards.

1:30 p.m.

Not much of a relaxing time at home because there is no school. I will go over to the kitchen to stir the beef stew we're having for supper and see if it needs more heat. The nice thing about our new Rational oven is that I do not need to cover anything with a lid or foil because it cooks with steam so there's no crust forming on top. I control the temperature by percentages, but I'm still new at it, and I'm learning as I go. It does help that two of my sisters are head cooks in other colonies, and one of them has been working for three or four years with a Rational. By now, she should know something about it, eh?

3:00 p.m.

The men have gone back to work, so the women folk will start to bathe their younger children and have showers themselves. It's time to dress in our newest dresses for church. Even I get to smell like perfume once in a while and not always like a fried chicken nugget. After I'm ready, I lay out fresh clothes for my family on their beds. My husband and sons wear white shirts and their best suits; my young daughters wear the green dresses that I finished sewing last week.

4:30 p.m.

I'm in the kitchen a bit later than usual, since everything is prepared. Once a week, on Saturday, we have a special dessert that is usually rich with cream and sugar, and lots of times has a shortbread crust or a bed of crumbs—pure calories. The assistant cooks choose whatever they want to make, and everyone always looks forward to a dandy dessert. They always check with me, and I will see that they have all the ingredients. This week they have chosen a dessert called Stripe-It-Rich. It's a crust of butter, almonds, and coconut, topped with a layer of whipped cream, cream cheese, and chocolate pudding with chunks of Skor chocolate bars. It takes a gallon of cream and a gallon of cream cheese. The girls increased the original recipe times seven. Portioning out the dessert is the job of the head cook, and I try to be extra careful and to cut perfect pieces and not wreck the slabs my assistants worked so hard to prepare. Being head cook has its privileges, and when the dessert is cut, I get to lick the knife. It tastes as delicious as it sounds!

5:00 p.m.

It's time for the *Nochesser* (after-eaters) to sit down and have our supper. We never rush today, because most head cooks don't go to church on Saturday evenings. With the extra time, I measure out the noodles for soup for Sunday dinner. It doesn't take long for a head cook to know who wants lots of noodles in their soup. I learned early on that the men want a bowl thick with noodles, much thicker than the women, who prefer lots of broth because they like to drink it.

Our church is attached to the dining hall and, when the service is over, the door will burst open and everyone will take their seats. The single girls will come straight to the kitchen to serve the food. I have lined up the serving dishes on the kitchen island for every adult according to age from oldest to youngest. We use one grouping of serving dishes for every three people. Maybe there is somebody missing today from one group, so I put less in those bowls. Or there may be a visiting member who decided to come and eat in the kitchen, so my assistants will tell me where he or she is seated, and I put more food in their bowls. Once again, I have to walk around and check to see that everybody has enough. I know beef stew with dinner buns is a favorite with the men on Saturday. They just inhale this meal. And guess what? When their shirts feel a little tight around the belly, they accuse their wives of using a smaller pattern size on their new shirts by mistake (nice excuse, eh!).

Supper is over, and I'm absolutely free this evening. No sewing, no cooking, just relaxing and visiting. My dear husband will take the menu sometime this evening and get out all the meat I need for next week from the freezer and place it into the walk-in chiller. After only a short time, he knows where everything is by heart, just like I do, so I don't even have to go with him anymore. He also fills up the coffee and sugar bins for the week. At first, he left a lot of droppings behind, but I gave him the what-for. Now he is much tidier, but I still do a quick sweep the next morning, because men seem to have eyesight problems in this department.

Colony Cleaning Notes—Spring Cleaning

Start Friday before Good Friday. All walls, ceilings, benches, appliances, and floors of all buildings must be thoroughly scrubbed down.

Friday   Kindergarten, Laundromat, Fridges, and Bakery. Take all baking pans, oven racks, large containers, and tubs down to slaughterhouse to be washed and sterilized. Assistant cooks will clean fryers and change lard

Sunday Evening   Girls wash kitchen canopy and the head cook's room. Assistant cooks wash stoves

Monday Morning   Start with sterilizing all the cutlery and dishes in the kitchen, clean all butter and syrup containers and all kitchen appliances, wash down church and basement.

Tuesday Morning   Wash down dining hall and kitchen

Wednesday   Cow barn

Thursday   Slaughterhouse

Fall cleaning starts Friday before last Tuesday of September, same as in spring

On first of July and just before Christmas, the grout in the kitchen tiles must be scrubbed with brushes

seven

Branching Out

*"No one with common sense
has ever fallen from Heaven."*

Taking a break from building a new colony

ONE OF THE SECRETS attributed to the Hutterites' success at establishing and retaining a collective way of life where others have failed is the Hutterite tradition of "branching out" when a colony exceeds one hundred members. Having only a certain number of people in each community is key to forming a cohesive group where everyone is accounted for and has a steady job within the cooperative. The broad rule of thumb for branching out is when a colony has a male workforce (age fifteen and over) of more than forty men, one elder told me. Planning ahead by at least twenty years is critical, he stresses. "If a colony goes in the ditch because of poor management or bad luck, then they can't branch out because they simply can't afford to." Colonies come to each other's aid within their own sects, but not all of them can be saved from foreclosure or bankruptcy.

I'm on my way to a new colony being built in Northern Alberta. It's been raining for weeks, and the back roads I'm traveling are waterlogged and difficult to navigate. I stop at farm houses along the way to ask for directions to the new Hutterite colony being built in the area. Local farmers nod knowingly and point me farther up the road, reconciled to the arrival of their unusual neighbor.

It was a different story altogether when the Hutterites first arrived in Canada in the early- to mid-twentieth century. General perceptions that they had an unfair advantage when it came to buying land because they didn't pay wages to their workers, coupled with their peculiar way of life, created widespread hostilities in the prairie provinces where Hutterites settled. Municipalities and governments sided with farmers who argued that they couldn't compete, giving rise to the creation of prejudicial laws and legislation restricting when, where, and if Hutterites could buy land. According to the website *Canada's Human Rights History,* dedicated to the history of human rights in Canada, Alberta's Land Sales Prohibition Act (1942–1947) and the Communal Property Act (1947–1973) are said to be "among the most blatant discriminatory pieces of legislation in Canadian history." They required Hutterites to seek permission from a provincial Communal Property Control Board for approval to buy land and prohibited colonies from locating within forty miles of each other. That all changed in 1972 when Peter Loughheed, the premier of Alberta, repealed the legislation, citing it in violation of the human rights code. Loughheed gave Hutterites the same opportunities to own land, property, and assets as anyone else. Other provinces followed suit.

"You're here!" shouts Tony Hofer when I arrive, as surprised as I am that I made it.

Tony is lumbering toward me with great strides, wrestling his rubber boots out of mud slicks every step of the way. When he removes his hat to scratch his forehead, I notice that he's entirely bald.

"I still have a beard," he reckons when I give him a startled look. Being bald in Hutterite culture is not an option, especially in the more traditional sects. If God gave you hair, you're expected to wear it unless, as in Tony's case, the good Lord had something to do with it. Even buzz cuts are frowned upon by the older generation. We don't want our boys looking like skinheads, one minister's wife told me.

The new colony sits on an acreage that once belonged to an old farmer whose son didn't share his father's passion for living off the land and sold out. The lonely farmhouse is getting a much-needed face-lift, and several new buildings have already gone up. Tractors and backhoes are expanding the yard for the homes and buildings yet to be constructed.

"Come, I'll show you what the boys are up to," he says, motioning for me to follow him.

Tony's in full throttle. He has a commanding presence and a loud voice. He talks as fast as he walks.

"Before we set up a new colony, we have to get permission from our own land committee. We got their approval, but we sure struck out with our women, because they think the new colony is too far from the mother colony. Five hundred miles is a long way, but whatya gonna do?" Tony opines, snapping one of his suspenders. "We have to go where we can find land, cuz we need at least 10,000 acres to make a go of it. Otherwise, forget it."

The Alberta land committee Tony is referring to consists of four Hutterite elders from the *Lehrerleut* sect and four from the *Dariusleut* sect. It was set up as a means for Hutterites to develop mutually beneficial relationships with municipalities and farmers who still have doubts about them. The land committee requires colonies that branch out to have the support of local municipalities and a viable water source before purchasing property.

"If you buy land where you don't have access to a river, it means you have to get an easement from the neighbor. We have a colony down south right now where the neighbor is refusing to give them an easement, and that's a big problem," says Tony, shaking his head.

"First we gotta have a means of supporting ourselves," he continues. "That's the priority around here. A year ago we built a carpentry and blacksmith shop so we could start constructing other things. And now the boys are building a dairy barn."

A cacophony of hammers grows progressively louder as we approach a clearing where half a dozen young men are putting up support beams for a huge wooden structure.

"On the mother colony, we have 11,000 laying hens and 600 cattle, with 70 milk cows for which we have a quota. We made the decision to leave the hens at the old place, and the new place will get the cows because the cow barn that we have there is just about ready for a major overhaul, whereas the chicken barn is in good shape. Splitting up the hens and the cows would not make sense, so we'll leave the chickens and take the cows. We branded cattle here last week. We already have some of our livestock grazing in the pasture beyond the tree line," he says, pointing south.

"Everything!" shouts a teenager when we come into view. He is standing in the mouth of a forklift nine feet in the air with two other teens wearing waist aprons. "We need more nails!"

"The boys call me Tony Everything," he explains, "because they say I think I know everything. Well, compared to those young bucks, I do," he says, unfazed.

Typically Hutterite colonies branch out every twenty-five to thirty years. In the past when the birth rate was significantly higher than it is today, it was more like every decade. As one example, I was born at New Rosedale Colony, which branched out to Fairholme Colony where I grew up, but by the time I was ten years old, Fairholme had already purchased the land for what would become Windy Bay Colony. The old colony is referred to as the mother colony and the new one is spoken of as the daughter colony, though they are also talked about as sister colonies.

"It takes at least two to three years and millions of dollars to build a new colony," says Tony, returning from replenishing his work crew. "If we have a crop failure or some other setback at the mother colony, it can take a lot longer than that.

"People think we have advantages that others don't have because we don't pay wages, but they don't take into account that we have to provide homes, food, medical, dental, and cradle-to-the-grave care for everyone in our communities. We don't own nearly as much land as people think we do."

According to 2006 Statistics Canada, Hutterites owned only 3 million of the 135 million acres of farmland on the prairie provinces. The average acreage owned per person by prairie farm families is 410, whereas the acreage owned per person on a Hutterite colony is 116. Another myth is the notion that Hutterites don't pay taxes. Far from being tax exempt, Hutterites pay more tax than the average citizen and considerably more than neighboring farmers. Hutterites don't collect unemployment insurance or social security benefits, despite having to pay into the programs like everyone else.

"Once we have our enterprises up and running, we build storage bins and a slaughterhouse. Then comes the community kitchen, bakery, and church, which are all one unit. After that the school, the kindergarten, and the family dwellings. They consist of three long row houses with seven or eight units to each row. When we have everything in place and enough work for everybody, then we split apart."

Tony and I fight our way past swarms of blackflies swirling around our heads. "I don't know why these devils love me so much," he says, his hands flailing.

"I read somewhere that blackflies are attracted to dark clothing," I tell him. "You'll have to start wearing pink."

"That would really impress my work crew," he chuckles.

"The rule is that the mother colony splits the assets with the new one in brotherly love. But sometimes brotherly love takes a back seat to greed, and that's when the trouble starts," Tony admits. "In the olden days, our elders just sat down at the kitchen table and divided the assets, but the more assets we accumulated, the more complicated things became. On occasion, it's led to so much bickering and fighting over who gets what, things got downright ugly, so now we get accountants involved. It's just human nature to want more than your share, I guess," he shrugs.

I ask Tony about claims that Hutterites don't participate in the local economy of the small communities around which they live.

"We have to be largely self-sufficient to make a go of it. Raising and butchering most of our own meat and having large vegetable gardens is something that we've always done. We try in our own way to benefit our small communities by helping the neighbors with combining, contributing to local food banks, or lending a hand in any kind of emergency, but when it comes to buying things from the store, most of the time we try to get the best deal, just like the next guy. For instance, the other day I got a call from Costco saying they just received a big shipment of toilet paper and we should send someone if we want in on the sale. A colony of 100 people uses a lot of this stuff, so I told the guy, 'We'll take 2,400 rolls but I can't get them until tomorrow so keep them in the loading dock 'til I get there.' He says, 'OK, what color would you like? The rolls come in pink, blue, and white.' I told him, 'Just give me white, we color them ourselves.' The guy nearly fell off his chair!" said Tony, giving his knee a slap.

"Well, that's all I know," he says abruptly. "I gotta get back to my work crew."

"I thought you were Tony Everything."

"Well, my wife's doing the cooking, and she'll be the first to tell you that's not true," he laughs, pointing to the door of a double-wide trailer.

"If you want to know everything, go see the women."

I step into a miniature Hutterite kitchen temporarily set up in a large trailer. The soup hens are boiling in a family-sized crock pot, and Selma, Tony's wife, is at the sink making cottage cheese. Her two young assistants, Lola and Lily, are shredding cabbage and carrots for the noon salad.

"Come in, come in," she waves, hurriedly wiping her dripping hands on her bib apron. "I've always wanted to meet you," Selma says, giving me a warm hug. "Ever since I read your *I Am Hutterite* book. I told Tony, I'd sure like to meet this girl, and now here you are."

"Here I am, a bona fide mud hen!" I tell her, pointing out the mud splats on my boots and outfit.

"Welcome to the club," she grins. "We can't remember what it's like to have sunshine anymore. I told the boys, if it ever gets nice again, I'll make them some cream-cheese pizza 'cause they love it."

Selma pours us a glass of iced coffee and leads me to the next room where seven tables are set up in rows. "This is our makeshift dining room," Selma explains, sliding down one of the benches as I take a seat opposite.

Selma and her sister-in-law Wilma, together with their husbands and children (Selma has six and Wilma five), have been here for the better part of two years, only occasionally going back home to the mother colony. Selma is the designated head cook and Wilma her right hand.

"Our young people of working age, the fifteen-and-ups, come here on a rotational basis because it's very exciting for them to come to the new colony. Our young women work here in the kitchen, and the guys work on construction. They enjoy getting away from home. But Wilma and I are in it for the long haul, or at least until the new colony is ready. Even though our families are with us, we miss the women back home a lot."

Selma slowly spins her coffee cup as she talks.

"The hardest part, as crazy as it sounds, is cooking for twenty when you're used to cooking for a hundred. Wilma and I are having a heck of a time downsizing our traditional recipes. Taking the colony bread recipe for forty loaves and reducing it to eight has been a real *kunst* (ordeal). We finally perfected it last week, and it turned out super," she says, patting her hand on the table, "but we are still working on some of the others.

"We get our meat and root vegetables like potatoes and carrots from the old colony, but we planted our own little garden this year so we could be more independent. The young girls helped us, and we have quite a nice plot on the go if it doesn't drown! Wilma and I have also decided to do some canning, so that will be another adventure in downsizing," she says, cocking her head to one side.

A chocolaty scent is drifting our way, and Wilma appears, cuddling a pie plate in a pair of yellow hot pads like it was a gift.

"I heard you were coming," she glows, "so I made you our 'recipe of the year.'"

"What is it?" I ask, my taste buds coming to life.

"I don't even know," Wilma confesses. "Our young girls are full of ideas, and we let them try a new dessert every week. This one was such a hit we just took to calling it 'recipe of the year.'"

She cuts into the dessert, and her knife gets trapped in the sticky caramel the cake is filled with. The pieces she dishes out are so moist they seem to expand in our plates.

"It ain't pretty, but it's so good," says Wilma, cleaning the knife with her fingers and enjoying a knot of caramel.

"Is there anything better than this?" she asks, her mouth full.

I give her a thumbs-up as I delight in the warm toffee, crunchy pecans, and rich chocolate. Every bite begs for more, and we shamelessly have two pieces before returning to our conversation.

"Every sect has a bit of a different tradition," Selma explains when I ask how they decide who goes where when the new colony is ready and it's time to branch out.

"Our custom [*Dariusleut*] is that our minister brings a piece of paper to the community kitchen with two columns. On one column is the senior minister's name and on the other the assistant minister's name.

"Every family writes their name beneath whichever minister they want to go with. It's called *Freiwillig* [free will]. Of course we all see who's going with whom, so we sign our names with the people we're closest to. Wilma and I will sign our names under the same minister because we are family, and we usually split up along family lines."

"Do you know by then who goes to which colony?"

"No, we don't. Sometimes the senior minister is given the first choice of staying or going with his group. But he is just as likely to put his name in the hat and let the good Lord decide. The draw is made in church, where two pieces of paper are put in a hat. One says *old colony* and the other *new colony*. It's a very exciting day for the community when the men come out of church and we find out for the first time what our future is going to bring."

"Is it difficult?" I inquire.

"Oh, yes. Our women have a strong bond, and for us to move so far apart from each other when we have lived and worked together most of our lives is going to be a heartbreaker. But in some colonies where people don't get along as well as we do, it can be a blessing. In that case they try and split things up between the 'get alongs' and the 'don't get alongs,' so both sides can have a fresh start," Selma says, finishing her coffee.

"What if the split is uneven and the workforce unevenly divided?"

"Oh, there is always some haggling that goes on. Every colony needs a certain balance of men, women, and children to make a go of it," she grins.

"How soon do the ones going to the new colony leave?"

"Usually it takes about two weeks and a lot of crying before all is said and done, and then those who are left behind can upgrade their own place or switch houses depending if they need a bigger or a smaller place."

While there are many similarities in the manner in which the three Hutterite sects establish a new colony, there is a real distinction between the more casual traditions of the *Dariusleut* and *Schmiedeleut* sects and the orthodox *Lehrerleut* when it comes to splitting up a community.

"Everybody packs," Paulina Basel (*Lehrerleut*) tells me over the phone.

"Even the ones staying behind?"

"Everybody," she says emphatically.

The lots aren't drawn until everybody is packed and ready.

"We don't have a say where we go. Immediate families stay together, and aging parents always go with the ones looking after them. Other than that, our ministers will divide the people as evenly as possible into two groups. We don't divide along family lines like the *Dariusleut*, so that means siblings with their own families may end up at different colonies. The senior minister draws first and whatever it says on his paper, that's final! No changing people back and forth.

"It usually works out very well, but sometimes it's hard on some families when they have to leave people they are really close to," Paulina Basel admits.

"The draw is usually made on Sunday afternoon, and all the women are watching out their window to see which minister will come out of the church first. The minister who has chosen the new colony always comes out of church first," she says, stopping to clear her throat.

"We are very organized," she continues. "We even get assistant cooks from other colonies to do the cooking. Every family that moves calls their own relatives from other colonies to come and help. Lots of trucks and vans are lined up outside the next morning, and in half a day nothing is left of the seven to eight families who used to live here. By noon, everybody who is going to the new colony is gone.

"So, since the rest of us are all in boxes too, we clean and renovate our homes. The colony provides us with supplies, and we get teenage girls and boys from other colonies to come help paint, varnish, or lay new linoleum. Young children are sent to relatives at other colonies, and in about ten days our homes are as fresh as new, we are unpacked and settled in, and we bring our children back home. Having a new house helps with the heartache of losing community members, and of course there's always the yak line," she laughs.

Back in the makeshift kitchen of the new colony, Selma is adding buckwheat to the *Gritz* soup she's making for the noon meal.

"So you and Wilma have no idea where you're going to end up?" I ask.

"If people knew where they were going, they might not work as conscientiously at the place where they won't end up. This way we are equally invested and give it our all at both places," Selma says as she carefully pours a bowl of beaten eggs in to the soup.

"I guess not knowing is the secret ingredient," she adds, giving me a wink.

- -

RECIPE OF THE YEAR

1 box Duncan Hines German Cake mix
14 ounce bag of caramels
½ cup evaporated milk
¾ cup melted butter
2 cups pecans
1 cup chocolate chips

Prepare cake mix as directed. Pour half the batter into greased 9- × 13-inch pan. Bake at 350°F for 15 minutes. Melt caramels with milk and butter over low heat, stirring constantly. Pour over cake and sprinkle with 1 cup pecans and 1 cup chocolate chips. Pour remaining batter over filling. Sprinkle with remaining nuts and bake for another 20 minutes.

- -

SELMA'S WHOLE WHEAT BREAD

7 cups warm water
¾ cup goose or chicken fat
2 cups cooked oatmeal (room temperature)
¼ cup bran
¼ cup molasses
3 tablespoons white sugar
3 tablespoons salt
8 cups whole wheat flour
3 tablespoons instant yeast
12 cups white flour

Put water in a large mixing bowl, add chicken fat, oatmeal, bran, molasses, sugar, and salt, then add whole wheat flour. On low speed beat till nice and smooth. Slowly add yeast, beat 5 minutes, then add remaining white flour. On low speed, mix dough for 10 to 15 minutes. Place on greased table, cut out 1¼ pound loaves. Cover with plastic. Let rise on table for 1 hour. Then roll with rolling pin to remove air pockets and shape into loaves. Place into 4- × 10-inch greased pans. Let rise 1½ hours. Bake in preheated oven at 375°F for 30 minutes until golden brown. Makes 8 loaves.

We Are Not Utopia: A Conversation with the *Prediger*

"I don't know where he went," the minister's wife, Elsie Basel, tells me when I arrive at her home for supper. Laundry is drying on the neighbor's wash line, and a crop of pleated skirts and cotton shirts flap lethargically in the sultry summer heat.

A week ago, I called Goliath Vetter, the *Prediger* minister at Evergreen Bay Colony, wanting to see him. He has no time to talk, he told me. He's too busy working the fields.

"But you're in your seventies," I protested. "Don't you catch a break?"

"Oh, I don't want one," he said certainly.

"I'm going to have to put my teeth in for that," he reports when I suggest having the conversation over the phone.

"Why don't you come and have supper with us next week and I'll make time," he says, offering a compromise.

"You have to nail that man down if you want to see him," says his wife contritely. "Don't worry; he'll be here for supper."

"Come, I'll show you my plants." She brightens. "That's my moses-in-the-cradle," she says, leading me to a houseplant. Sleek sword-shaped leaves with deep green tops and rich purple undersides frame white lily-like florets tucked into purple bracts. "Isn't it gorgeous?" she exclaims.

I have to agree. The plant has a tropical feel, and its dramatic foliage is eye catching.

"I got it from one of our English neighbors," she says, pleased. "We baked the buns when her husband died, and she wanted to say thank-you.

"And this here is my lipstick plant," she says, pointing to it.

Bright red flowers with yellow throats bud in a cavity resembling a tube of lipstick twisted from its case. I smile at the improbability of Elsie Basel wearing lipstick, much less the vibrant red of the florets.

"Hallo, hallo," Goliath Vetter announces himself, disappearing into the bathroom to wash up.

Elsie Basel pours us small tumblers of icy and invigorating dandelion wine just as a teenage girl arrives from the community kitchen with covered dishes containing our supper.

Goliath Vetter emerges, his thick, dark hair freshly combed and parted down the middle. He is a short and stocky workhorse of a man. His dusty black trousers are held up by suspenders and the sleeves of his checkered brown shirt are rolled up, exposing big bony wrists. He shakes my hand vigorously. His wide smile reveals a rather unfortunate set of dentures. They are much too big and when I, in true Hutterite fashion, tell him so, he admits he got them "on sale."

"*Voter, ips der zok.* Dad, I told you this!" his wife agrees.

"I'm hungry, let's eat," he says cheerfully. We all clasp our hands as he recites the table prayer. Elsie Basel ladles hot *Milich Geschtal* into plain green bowls and fills our plates with steamed rice, baked parsnips, corn on the cob, and grilled lamb loin chops. The *Milich Geschtal* consists of ragged bits of pasta cooked in hot milk. Theys are as chewy as an oatmeal cookie and the salty milk broth smooth and soothing. I am a fan of parsnips and an even greater fan of lamb. The tiny lamb loins Elsie Basel has put on my plate resemble miniature T-bone steaks. They are butter soft with such a delicious bold taste I almost forget why I'm here.

"I've been minister since 1969," Goliath Vetter says, initiating our Q and A, and I take my cue.

What is the most important attribute a Hutterite minister should have?

A minister's job is to lead his people and leading by example is the best way to lead. If there is a problem, you have to deal with it and convince that person to come back to the fold and not to go astray. In our sermon yesterday, we heard that you go to the brother and you say to him, listen, this is not quite right what you're doing and if he admits that he is in the wrong, you try and catch him early so he can make it right. I'm with the people ninety percent of the time, and I think a good minister has to spend a lot of time working with the people and being around them so you know what's going on. My wife says I'm gone ninety percent of the time and maybe that's why we get along so good! But it's true, I do travel quite a lot because I have to go and help out with colonies where there's a lot of friction. I love to take my wife along because she gives me good advice, but she doesn't like to travel. She's a homebody. When I leave, my assistant minister takes full responsibility. He's in charge when I go away. That's what he's there for.

What do you see as the biggest challenges facing the Hutterite community?

In my opinion, it's lack of communication. If the colony leaders don't communicate effectively with each other, it causes huge problems. Everybody on the colony has a job: one is the sheepherder, one's the hog man, one man is the feed boss, one is the turkey guy, the horse guy, the cattle guy … if one hand doesn't know what the other one is doing, you're in trouble. The people on the ground should be in regular contact with the two *Prediger*, the financial boss, and the farm steward. We all have to know what's going on, and if someone just goes ahead and does things on his own, it's inappropriate. Most of the time if the colony doesn't get along, it's because the men are doing their own thing and not consulting with each other. We have a meeting here every morning, and we discuss all the important issues.

So what did you discuss this morning?

Well, we used to take our sheep up into the mountains. Years ago, the government had trouble keeping the weeds down around trees that they planted by dropping five-inch seedlings from an airplane. When the seedlings started growing in the fall, they were choked out by the weeds. But a sheepherder figured out that sheep will not eat the trees, just the weeds. So he did a test on 200 acres and proved to the government that it was true. A fellow phoned us and told us they need sheep up there to get rid of the weeds, and he said he's looking for sheep. They want to take our sheep all summer and bring them back in the fall. So our sheepherder said he would give the guy 600 sheep, and I asked him, Well how many does he want? and the boss said he wants 900, so I told him go tell the sheepherder to give him 900. It doesn't cost us anything, and it frees the sheepherder to do other work and we got lots to do. He doesn't have to be out there looking after sheep. The government used to pay us twenty-five dollars a sheep, but then they ran out of money, so now they'll only pay us five to ten dollars, which is alright too because we want our country's trees to grow. What they did at one time is put students out there to do the weeding, but when it rained the students couldn't go out, and it rained so often it wasted a lot of time and money. But sheep don't mind the rain.

How did you end up at this colony? Were you born here?

No, no. When we branched out from the old colony in 1977, I was convinced to come here. I was the junior minister at the time, and the senior minister asked me to go voluntarily. I said, If the people who wrote their names on my paper agree, I'll do it. Otherwise we would have had to pull lots and let the good Lord decide. But the people agreed, so we went by choice. I knew the place, and I had managed it while we were building it up, so I felt comfortable to go. But I also had an ulterior motive. My father had wanted the land to this colony for a long time, but because of government restrictions against Hutterites at the time, we were not allowed to buy it. Thankfully after the restrictions were lifted, my father's dream was realized.

We consult with the municipality and with the neighbors, and if they are both in agreement that we can buy the land and build a Hutterite colony, then we are satisfied. It's not the law, but, as a good neighbor, you know you have a better chance of making a living as a colony than a farmer, so you have to consider individual farmers. He's trying to get his son going too, so we bend over backwards to try and please our neighbors, and it has been very profitable for us to create good relationships. The Bible says love thy neighbor as you love thyself. I was just tested the other day when one of our English neighbors phoned over and said they needed water. Well, we're very busy these days, but I said to her, I'll get you water. If you love your neighbor, you have to help them, that's all there's to it.

Why are you still driving a tractor? Shouldn't you be easing into retirement?

Our ministers don't get paid, but the welfare of his people is on his shoulders, so most Hutterite ministers, unless they are too frail, work. Even the apostle Paul worked. He was a man of God, but he also weaved carpets.

Some colonies are seeing many of their young people leave the colony. The percentage of young men leaving is on the rise. How do you account for that?

Lack of communication, lack of faith, and lack of work. You have to have faith in your heart and take it seriously. Idleness is the devil's best ally. I think it's better to have too much work than not enough because young people, until they come to a place of accountability where they have a good conscience about what is right and wrong and want to be baptized, require nurturing and encouragement. It's important to give them work so that they are busy and become knowledgeable and responsible. You can't just talk to young people. You've got to keep them busy because it keeps them out of trouble. You can't control young minds because they have their own ideas, but if you teach them that they have value and that you need them, it helps them through those uncertain years. I worked with a young fifteen-year-old all day Saturday raking hay for the baler. It was amazing how well we worked together.

But don't both the men and the women work excessively hard on a Hutterite colony?

We used to. Our ancestors did. But we are so automated already: our feed systems in the barns are automated, we have robots milking our cows, and our combines practically drive themselves!

What about the women?

Every time we get something, they get something too. They have a Rational oven that turns itself off and on and is completely self-cleaning. We've just installed a $40,000 dishwasher in our colony's kitchen. We have potato diggers and carrot diggers … you name it. These days we're far more likely to die of overeating than overworking!

How do you deal with disciplinary issues on a colony?

First, discipline on a colony is a lot more serious once you are a baptized member than if you are not. Once you have made your vows to God and the church, a higher standard of behavior is expected of you.

If you see that someone has a problem, you have to go to them and talk with them. Then if he doesn't listen, you take two or three other brothers, and if he still doesn't listen then, you go to the council and put him in *Unfrieden* (out of peace), which essentially means to excommunicate him. Some try to punish the person right away, but that is not right. The right thing is to give the man a chance to make things right, but if he doesn't, then proceed with excommunication. In order to be reinstated into the community, he has to admit his sin, to publicly apologize to colony members, and say that he is ready to receive his due.

Say he committed adultery, was physically abusive, or got drunk and made a mess of things, then his status is reduced to that of an unbaptized member. He eats with the young boys, he works with the young boys, and he is treated like a boy because he is not acting like a man. But when he comes and asks for forgiveness and seeks reconciliation, he must first accept his punishment.

When he accepts his punishment, he eats by himself. He is removed from his family and lives in a separate place in the community, and he is isolated. But we provide work for him ... a corner in the shop where he'll do some kind of a job. A man has to do something. He can't just sit and look out the window. The purpose of this is so that he can think things over and consider the consequences of his actions. After a time alone, he is reconciled and returned to his family and the community. There is no set time as to how long it lasts. It depends entirely on the person, whether they are truly remorseful and willing to repent.

Are the women disciplined in this manner as well?

Yes, all baptized members are disciplined in the same way, but the wrongdoings generally differ between male and female members of the community. The women usually have some kind of cause, and disciplining them can be a nightmare. Generally speaking, men who get in trouble surrender more quickly. The women don't. They are fiercely stubborn and tougher to deal with. If they can't have their way, they will have their say!

How is the computer age changing the Hutterite culture?

The computer age is a problem for us. We have to give the young a little bit of leeway. We won't stop the computer age, but we have to be very careful how much we allow it to take over our lives. We do so much of our business on the computer, it's both friend and foe. Our policy is we don't want computers in individual homes. We're very careful. There are quite a few of our teenaged boys leaving, but we are able to keep more of them than the *Lehrerleut* because we allow them a bit more independence. You have to let them have a chance, give them some freedoms. For example, we let our young boys go to town for supplies on their own without supervision. We say, Boys, take these potatoes to the IGA in town, but we expect you back at a certain time. They appreciate being trusted and they're proud of that.

Young people are like wild horses: if you hold the reins too tight, they'll break loose and get away, but if you give them too much freedom, you'll never train them. You have to find the balance.

What do you say to those people who think Hutterites are trying to create some type of Utopia?

That we have failed miserably, that's what! We are like everyone else, and, let me tell you, we have our share of problems both great and small. We suffer from the same human conditions that other people suffer—greed, selfishness, lack of true Christian love. It is so important that we remain humble. God has richly blessed many of our communities, but success is more dangerous than failure. You get puffed up and proud. You really have to watch yourself.

Sure, there are things I am grateful for. There has never been a murder on a Hutterite colony in all the 150 years we have lived in the United States and Canada. Our divorce rate is nil. We don't have a significant drug problem. Alcoholism and gambling are more of a problem, and we try to deal with these matters on a case-by-case basis and by the grace of God to help those who are involved in this sort of destructive behavior. We have some very bad situations just like out in the world.

Do you think that the Hutterite culture will survive the next 50 to 100 years?

If you look at our history, it is only by the grace of God that we are here at all. And if we do survive for the next century, it will only be by the grace of God. The challenges ahead are enormous. Only God knows the answer to this question.

eight

The Leftovers

"Luck and glass are equally fragile."

Mourners on their way to the colony cemetery

"HE STOPPED THE SWATHER and died," my friend Hilda, the head cook from Brent Colony, tells me over the phone. "*Mir welln nit hobn dos es woares, ober is es.* We don't want it to be true, but it is."

Jamie, the thirty-two-year-old colony mechanic, had died from an apparent heart attack. He had been enlisted to assist the men with the harvest and was found with his right hand still on the gearshift and his head slumped against his chest. "He didn't even have time to turn off the engine," a shocked Fritz Wurtz told the colony boss. Ironically, Jamie's mother had also died of a heart attack while holding him in her arms when he was a baby. He had slipped away as silently and as suddenly as she had.

Jamie's loss to the community could not compare to the loss to his family. He and Adina had been married for eight years, and they had four young girls ranging in age from seven months to seven years. This week had been Adina's cook week, and she saw him off that morning, pressing a thermos of coffee into his hands.

"When I married Jamie, everybody told me I had to take really good care of him because he grew up without a mother," a heartbroken Adina told the colony women. "I didn't realize we would have such a short time together."

When a colony member dies, among the first to be notified is the head cook, who immediately begins preparing for the huge influx of visitors who will arrive for the wakes and funeral. Unlike weddings, where invitations are necessary, funerals allow anyone with a connection to the deceased to come and pay their respects. While an elderly member might draw a smaller crowd of bereaved friends and relatives, a tragic death like Jamie's can bring 700 mourners for each of the two wakes and as many as 1,000 for the funeral.

"We're all in shock," Hilda concedes, "so tonight's supper will be simple. We're having sausages, fried rice, and coleslaw." One of the liabilities of being head cook is that Hilda has to announce the death of a member over the kitchen's intercom system. "I just couldn't do it. When the boss called me, I told him that. He said he couldn't either. We were both so sad. I made a mistake last time," Hilda sheepishly admits. "The boss called to say Aaron Vetter had died so I broadcast it, and not two minutes later, Aaron Vetter called and said, 'Don't bake the buns; I'm not dead yet!' I nearly fell over. It was Darren Vetter, the old hog man, who had died. I really blew it that time," she says, retying her *Tiechel*.

Hilda has mobilized her counterparts from nearby colonies who will be pitching in by baking bread, buns, cakes, and cookies.

They will also prepare meat and side dishes to help feed the 300 or so guests who will descend by nightfall, increasing the size of Brent Colony to a thousand. She tells me that Buffalo Butte Colony is sending over sixty pounds of their homemade sausage, forty loaves of banana bread, and thirty-five quart jars of canned peaches. The head cook at Ruby River Colony was asked to take care of the 700 carrot, date bran, and saskatoon muffins that will be served with hard-boiled eggs and cheese for breakfast over the course of three days.

Hilda is responsible for creating the menus and advising the colony boss of the extra groceries that will have to be purchased. Just for the wakes, she estimates that they will need twelve large hams, eight blocks of sliced cheese, two cases of lettuce, two cases of Colombian coffee, one case of celery, and two big bags of peppermint candy for breath fresheners. Hilda also requested two cases of paper cups for coffee and two cases of paper plates.

She has decided on burgers, salad, cold veggies, and dip for tomorrow's noon meal, and on the second day, the women will roast ninety chickens and make fresh noodle soup. Suppers will take advantage of the colony's abundant garden produce and well-stocked meat freezers: lamb shank and mashed potatoes with corn on the cob for one meal, and beef stew, roasted potatoes, and steamed beets for the other. With all the extra visitors, Hilda expects to feed people in shifts.

Adina does not have to worry about booking a church, picking a plot, choosing a casket, or paying for the funeral. While the head cook organizes the meals, the boss enlists the carpenter at Ruby River to make a pine coffin for Jamie. Some of the younger women prepare Adina's home for the inevitable crush of visitors—changing bed linens and washing floors and furniture. Adina is relieved of all her work indefinitely, and her immediate and extended families will rush from their colonies to be by her side. Nearby colonies will provide accommodation and meals for mourners coming from out of province.

The colony machine shop often serves as a venue for funerals, but the boss wisely decided to rent an enormous white tent, which is almost full when I arrive for the wake. A handful of people from neighboring farms who have come to pay their respects are wearing jeans and colored T-shirts, severing the uniformity of tailored black jackets and hundreds of *Tiecheln* falling in V-shaped symmetry down women's backs. I find a seat at the back as the colony shoemaker searches for more chairs. "I wish that was me, all stretched out like that," he says, crestfallen. "I'm old and tired. I wouldn't mind going home."

Through the open tent flaps, a late-August sunset washes the sky in oranges, reds, and golds. A shaft of light falls on Jamie's open coffin in the middle of the room; grease stains are still visible on his dinner plate–sized hands, which days ago were fixing machinery. His head is resting on a feather pillow, and he is wearing his Sunday best—a white shirt, suspenders, black pants, and white socks—the color of angels.

It was once the domain of Hutterite women to prepare a body for burial, but since the 1960s, the law requires embalming to be

Everyone looks after the graves of their loved ones,
located on the outskirts of every community

done at funeral homes. Jamie's body will rest in the living room of his home and be carried to and from the memorials by the men of the colony.

The colony minister clears his throat and leads us in a traditional mourning song, composed by martyrs of the early Hutterite church. It is lengthy and haunting, a testament to our ancestors who sang the songs from prison cells, waiting for their death. Between songs, each of the six ministers sitting at the head table rises with words for the family. "We cannot argue with God. He doesn't tell us how we die, when we die, why we die, or where we die. We must accept his will," says one *Prediger*. "Adina, we will look after you and your daughters," she is promised by another. "We will feed and clothe you, and we will do our best to comfort and support you."

The wake began at seven o'clock and will end at midnight. As darkness settles on the colony, the women unload tubs of fresh ham sandwiches, coffee, orange juice, and oatmeal cookies on tables set up just outside the tent. The welcomed break gives mourners an opportunity to view the body and offer condolences to the family.

Every colony has its own graveyard, and every family tends to the grave of their loved ones. On my way here, I passed the small cemetery on the fringe of the community, which will become Jamie's final resting place. I remember Saturday afternoons when I was a young girl in Fairholme and *Oma* would summon me from play to go with her to the colony cemetery. We made our way to my brother Renie's grave; nearby lay *Oma*'s husband, *Opa*.

Death was something that *Oma* longed for. She and *Opa* had fled Russia, but most of their children had starved to death or had gone missing in the turmoil of the 1917 revolution. Her life was one of perpetual longing to be reunited with them. After pulling the weeds and watering the flowers around the graves, she would stand back and contemplate the unclaimed spot next to *Opa* that one day would be hers. A single, agonizing wail from an ache so deep and a pain so wide escaped from within her, joining the hum of bees and the sweltering heat of the afternoon sun. When the grief had settled, she lifted her apron and wiped her burning face. Tucking loose strands of her white hair back into her kerchief, she turned to me and reached for my hand as we walked out of the cemetery in silence.

At Bright Star Colony in Montana, Eva and Walter Hofer are sitting on a bench under the shade of an old oak tree just outside the community kitchen. Although their faces are weathered and their hands rest on sturdy *Stabellen* (wooden canes), they exude contentment.

The Hofers have been married for sixty years, but they will never have to worry about moving to a nursing home or downsizing when one of them dies. On the colony, it is considered a privilege to look after the sick and elderly, who age with dignity and are given special status. Daughters-in-law and granddaughters clean the Hofers' home, wash their floors, and bring them food if they choose not to go to the community dining room. Strong families mean a strong community, and women who marry to other colonies are given up to two weeks a year to go home to visit parents, no matter how great the distance. Should either of the Hofers become too frail, their caregivers will be a continual rotation of their three daughters-in-law who live on the colony and their five daughters brought in from other colonies for three-week stretches. Those daughters, in turn, will have their children looked after by in-laws and other members of their communities.

The *Kronka Kechin* (special cook) is assigned to cook special meals for the elderly whose palates often prefer old-fashioned favorites like soups and *Totsch*. "We love potatoes," Eva Basel tells me. "And we like them fried in a little goose lard, don't we, Father?" she editorializes, patting her deaf husband on the knee.

When Eva and Walter pass away, they will be spared the embarrassment of having their children fight over their bank account or personal belongings. Their house belongs to the community, and they leave nothing of significant value like artwork or fine china. Small remembrances such as needlework, houseplants, books, and leftover fabric will be shared among the children. Often it is the youngest child, rather than the oldest, who is entitled to the most significant knickknack, like a sweetheart hankie.

When children leave the colony to live in the outside world, the family unit is fractured, and the loss can be especially great to a mother. That's what prompted my mother's widowed older sister, Anna Basel, to leave Deerboine Colony and move to Winnipeg to be with her children. She had many health challenges and, before she died at the age of seventy-nine, she had one request: to be buried next to her husband in the Deerboine Cemetery. The colony hierarchy agreed to the burial, but the funeral service would have to take place in Winnipeg.

Her memorial was English dipped in Hutterite. After a moving eulogy, her brother Darius from New Rosedale Colony marched to the front of the church, unannounced, and stopped next to his sister's open casket. "I would like the remaining sisters to come and stand beside me," he instructed.

The request was unconventional, but my mother and her sister, Sana Basel, hobbled to the front. For the first time in many years, the siblings stood side by side, a remnant of the once-iconic Maendel family. Their grandfather, Jakob Maendel, was among the first group of Hutterites that sailed from Russia to America in 1874, seeking a life free from religious oppression. Their father, Joseph Maendel, was a respected leader at Old Rosedale who managed the largest and most successful Hutterite colony in Manitoba. My aunts were forces of nature who left an indelible mark on this world, and my uncle Darius had always seemed larger than life with his dark beard and watchful eyes. Now they stood together with lined faces and diminished bodies, witness to countless bereavements over the years—husbands, wives, sisters, brothers, and children. They had swallowed the bitter pill of loss and survived.

"We are the leftovers," Darius Vetter declared with a sweep of his hand. A soft rumble rose from the audience. "And Sana Basel," he predicted in his perfectly frank and open Hutterite manner, "you're next."

The congregation froze, but his oldest sister nodded. "Yes, yes, yes," Sana Basel agreed, excited about the prospect of Heaven and practical about the odds of getting there. "I'm next."

Elderly Hutterites are comfortable with the inevitability of death and consider it a reward for a long life well lived. In contrast to seniors in the outside world, who often feel isolated and vulnerable, their sunset years are fulfilled and happy, and their final rite of passage is supported and shouldered by the entire community.

Funeral Rules

- All women wash dishes after all meals
- If colony cleaning happens to be the same day as the funeral, it goes to the following week (same days)
- No kindergarten the day of the funeral
- If somebody dies on a Friday and the bakers of this week are finished baking, the next-week bakers bake the funeral buns
- Daughters-in-law are required to do their work (depends on situations)
- Clean up the dishes after dinner (funeral day), and the rest of the cleanup is right after the funeral lunch. Wash all floors on hands and knees (all women except the cooks)
- Parents, sisters, and children don't have to work the whole day after the funeral

My father, Ronald Dornn, died in 2010 after a ten-year battle with dementia. He was eighty-seven years old, and it was agonizing to watch his decline. I was in the doctor's office with my mother when he was diagnosed. We sat in a gloomy, windowless room in a strip mall while the white-coated doctor asked my father a series of questions.

"When is your birthday?"

"April 26, 1923," my mother answered for him.

"Who is the queen of England?"

"Queen Elizabeth," my mother interjected.

"*Please*, Mrs. Dornn," said the exasperated physician, directing his next question squarely at my father. "What is the difference between a cabbage and a cow?"

My father began to laugh. He had been the cow man at Fairholme Colony for ten years, and his diligence earned the colony the largest milk quota in the province. Every morning he awoke at five o'clock and walked to the barn in the dark. He loved the quiet, magical way that the sun rose and pulled back the curtains on the day. He considered it a blessing to be a spectator to such splendor and to be serenaded by the birds. "You're a doctor, and you don't know the difference between a cabbage and a cow?!" he replied in astonishment. His answer was the one light moment in a day that ended with a diagnosis as dark as the doctor's office.

As a young Hutterite girl, my mother had been taught the importance of caring for the elderly, and even when the load with my father became too much, she refused to put him in a care home. She insisted on washing, dressing, and feeding him, leaving her housebound most of the time. She would sing with him and read him stories from the Bible or *Reader's Digest*. In the summers, she made sure he didn't miss out on his favorite food, like sweet corn, plump Bing cherries, and *Schtrankel Soupen* (string bean soup) with sour cream. When she occasionally slipped away to a restaurant without him, she would wrap a takeaway morsel of Kentucky Fried Chicken, crisp wontons, or anything with a crunch and bring it to him.

Their lives became a cycle of good and bad days. On the colony, the added burden of shopping for groceries, cooking, and driving to medical appointments would have been assumed by somebody else. Although my brothers, who lived nearby, and my sisters and I, who live in different provinces, tried to support our mother, it was strenuous trying to juggle our parents' needs with our own obligations.

On the twenty-second of July, just as dawn was breaking, my father died in hospital after an eight-week round-the-clock vigil.

"He's gone to milk the cows," I said to my mother when she called me with the news of his death. In the final years of his illness, he was always asking after his cows.

The day of his funeral, the weather was hot and humid. Voluminous clouds offered little relief from the sun's brilliance. Fairholme and New Rosedale Colony sent large blocks of cheese and dozens of fresh buns as a tribute. My youngest brother found a country graveyard near my parents' home, and my eldest brother arranged for Deerboine Colony to make a beautiful maple coffin. We stood by the open grave in the shadow of a giant oak tree where five new shovels pierced a mound of freshly dug earth. In Hutterite tradition, my brothers began the process of burying their father. The shovels were then passed from person to person so everyone could participate in returning him to the land that he loved.

In 1969 when my dad took us off the colony, it changed the course of our lives, but it didn't change our birthright. The Klanaschuel Ankela's simple reply to the young boy who asked who I was said it all. "*Sie ket tzu uns.* She belongs to us," she told him. My DNA will forever trace me to the womb of my ancestors, a remarkable people deemed by historians as the finest example of community life in the modern world.

Funeral Menu for Edward Wipf

Joan and Sally baked 6 pails of buns

Shirley and Becky cooked on Sunday

Audrey and Lena cooked on Monday and Tuesday

FIRST DAY

Supper	144 smokies, 14 quarts of fried rice, salad
Evening Lunch	Bung sausage, summer sausage, hard cheese, bread, butter, mayonnaise
	No paper plates
	1 tub of sandwiches sent to the home of the relatives

SECOND DAY

Breakfast	6 flats of scrambled eggs, cheese slices, bread, jam
Noon Meal	200 pounds of fryers, steamed carrots, broccoli, cauliflower (1 tub each), green salad
Supper	90 pounds of cubed steak, baked hash browns, veggie plate with dip
Evening Lunch	Black Forest ham, pepperoni sausage, cheese slices, bread, butter

THIRD DAY

Breakfast	6 flats of cooked eggs, 30 pounds bacon, bread, jam
Noon Meal	200 pounds beef stew, 4 tubs of potatoes, coleslaw
	Put water on table at all meals
To Take to Individual Homes	Women on bake week fill 100 bags of buns. Slice 54 pounds of hard cheese, 40–50 pounds of ham, 20 pounds of pepperoni sausage

Leah's Diary

Sunday, February 22
5:45 a.m.

I wake up and wonder why the alarm clock didn't go off, but I soon realize that it's Sunday and I can sleep for a few minutes longer.

The assistant cooks boil some wieners and make scrambled eggs for breakfast, which we'll have with buns and coffee.

6:15 a.m.

I get up and dress in a much more relaxed way than any other day. When I do go to the kitchen, I measure out some dry ingredients and some spices that I'll need to marinate the meat for the Monday noon meal. After having breakfast with my assistants, I go back home to be with my family for an hour until church starts. It doesn't take long for the mind to wander and for some interesting recipes to crowd out the sermon.

10:45 a.m.

Church is over, so I hurry home and change out of my good clothes and go off to the kitchen. My assistants make sure the soup broth is boiling hot when I arrive, so I just need to pour it onto the noodles I measured out in bowls yesterday.

Today the assistants and I eat after the adults, when the school-age children eat. After dinner is quiet time for everybody in the community until after *Lunche*.

❧

3:00 p.m.

We've had our naps, relaxed, and had a nice family break. I am going back to work. Today we are having chicken wraps for supper, so I'll start by grilling the chicken meat. The assistant cooks for next week come over to the kitchen to see if they can do any prep work for Monday. I ask them to cut meat into strips for pork in a teriyaki sauce. Tomorrow we are having meat loaf and mashed potatoes for the noon meal, so I mix the beef, bread crumbs, eggs, onions, and spices and set the mix in the walk-in fridge.

❧

4:00 p.m.

I'm done grilling the meat for the chicken wraps. We buy our tortilla wraps, because we can never get them to turn out like the ones in the store. I asked the boss for 120 on my grocery list last week because the men like to have two each. If they don't eat it for supper, they can take it home for later.

❧

4:30 p.m.

The rush to get everything done is over now. We are ready to ring the bell for first call. It is a bit earlier today,

but church will be at 5:00 p.m. tonight instead of 5:30
or 6:00 p.m. This gives me a nice long evening to do my
laundry. Before one week has ended, the other begins. All
that changes are my assistant cooks. I always have to adapt
to the new ones and pray that we'll work well together
for the whole week, because the secret to being a good
head cook is getting along with everybody, which is not
always easy.

By the way, I finished the white shirts for my men, and
they look good.

nine

❧

Hutterite Recipes

RECIPES FROM LEAH'S COOKBOOK

Hutterites have a rich oral tradition. History, songs, and stories are all passed down orally, so it should come as no surprise that the way the women cook is passed down the same way. When Leah became head cook, she relied on her predecessor as well as the older women in the community to guide her. She admits to needing a lot of sticky notes that first year because, while her cookbook generally gave her amounts, sometimes it simply said *a fist full of salt* or *the blue bowl full of eggs*. The directions are often vague or left out entirely. This may feel like a challenge to those of you who know their way around a kitchen, but for others, like me, it's pure entertainment, especially the *Sauer Kraut* recipe.

After we left the colony, my mother, through trial and error, downsized colony recipes, which I have included at the end of the book for you to try.

But first, for your reading pleasure, are extracts from Leah's cookbook to give you an idea what it takes to feed a community of one hundred members year-round.

Enjoy!

- -

GRAUA KNEDEL MIT SCHMAGUS

(Gray Dumplings with White Sauce *also known as washing-machine dumplings*)

80 cups finely ground potatoes	10 cups flour
28 cups mashed potatoes	1 cup salt

Place ground potatoes in cheesecloth bags and wash with warm water and then with cool water (a little lemon juice in the cool water is helpful) until starch is washed out. Drain well. Spin dry in spin cycle of your washing machine. Be sure cheesecloth bags have a good tight knot.

Mix ingredients together and hand roll into plump shapes. Steam for 20 minutes in a food steamer.

Schmagus *White Sauce:*

100 cups milk	¾ cup salt
10 cups flour	½ cup butter

Melt the butter. Add the milk, flour, and salt, and bring to gentle boil until it thickens. Pour a layer of sauce on the bottom of a baking pan. Add dumplings and pour another layer of sauce on top. Bake at 275°F for 45 minutes.

KATUFEL TOTSCHELEN

(Potato Pancakes with Cream Sauce)

8 cups ground potatoes	2 tablespoons salt
16 eggs	2 cups hot milk
5 tablespoons flour	

Mix potatoes, eggs, flour, and salt. Add milk and beat with fork. Ladle onto a hot skillet oiled with goose lard. Serve with cream sauce.

Cream Sauce:

6 cups milk	⅓ cup salt
3 cups cornstarch	½ cup butter

Cook until it thickens.

SCHUTEN KRAPFLEN

(Deep-Fried Cottage-Cheese Pockets)

20 pounds cottage cheese	1 bowl onions
18 eggs	9 cups sugar
2 bowls bread crumbs	3 tablespoons salt
1 pound butter	

Dough:

10 cups water
4 eggs
2 tsp salt

Enough flour until sides of the mixing bowl come clean.

Saute onions in butter until lightly brown and add the rest of the filling ingredients.

Then spoon onto dough jackets. Pinch together edges. Cook in water or steam for 10 minutes, then in fryer until golden brown at 300°F. Serve with whipped or sour cream and pancake syrup.

෬ SOUPS ෬

CABBAGE *VORSCH*

(Cabbage Soup)

1 big bowl cut-up cabbage
As much water as needed
1 gallon jar tomatoes
A little salt
A little sugar
Half gallon of cream

- -

NUCKELA

(Dumpling Soup)

Serves 70.

3 pounds butter
12 cups eggs
5 quarts flour
3 tablespoons baking powder
3 tablespoons salt
Large kettle of chicken broth

Whip butter until it is very fluffy, then add lightly beaten eggs. Sift together flour, salt, and baking powder. Work into egg and butter mix just until well blended. Do not overwork. Drop into boiling broth using ice cream scoop. Cover and let boil over medium heat for 15 minutes. If you prefer firmer dumplings, add 2 more cups of flour.

- -

NUCKELA FOR NEW MOTHERS
(not quite as rich)

2 cups butter
3½ to 4 cups flour
10 eggs
1 gallon chicken broth

Beat butter to a cream, add eggs and blend. Add flour and mix together by hand. Make balls with ice cream scoop. When broth boils, add *Nuckela* balls and simmer for 15 minutes. Add fresh parsley or dill if you have it on hand.

- -

MAULTOSCHE
(Big Cheek Soup)

Filling:

50 eggs
5 pounds butter
4 large onions
5 loaves bread crumbs
Salt to taste
Chicken broth

Cream butter and add eggs. Beat well. Add cut-up onions and bread crumbs and mix well. Put generous spoonful into dough pockets and drop into boiling chicken broth. Let simmer for 10–15 minutes.

Dough for Maultosche:

10 cups flour + 2 cups more if dough is too soft
2 cups melted margarine
5 eggs
7½ tablespoons sour cream
3½ cups water

- -

Fleish *Krapflen*

1 level big bowl-on-wheels of hog brain and pork meat
4 loaves of bread
Salty soup broth

Grind twice with 32 (3/16) inch grinding plate

We need 17 pounds for 1 meal.

Dough for Fleish Krapflen

5 cups white and 5 cups whole wheat flour
   + 2 cups more if dough is too soft
2 cups melted margarine
5 eggs
7½ tablespoons sour cream
3½ cups water

Make dough a few hours before making the filling. Make into perogies. Fry slowly in deep fat. Double the recipe for 140 people.

- -

Noodles

30 pounds flour
16 pounds eggs
2 cups water

Water is to be weighed together with the eggs so water and eggs make 16 pounds together. Let stand at least 2 hours before making noodles. Cover with heavy plastic and pack down with feet.

- -

TOMATO SOUP

1½ cups flour
4 cups cold milk
20 cups milk, heated
16 cups tomato juice
3 teaspoons baking soda
3 teaspoons celery salt
1 cup butter
1 cup cream

Mix flour with 4 cups of cold milk to make a smooth paste. Add to heated milk. In a separate bowl, mix tomato juice, soda, and celery salt. Mix flour and milk paste with juice mixture and add butter. Boil for 1 minute. Reduce heat and keep warm. Add 1 cup of cream just before serving.

- -

GRITZ SOUPEN

(Buckwheat Soup)

20 cups buckwheat
15 eggs

Mix together in large bowl and let set for 1 hour before putting it into simmering chicken broth. Slowly stir the buckwheat mixture to keep it from sticking to the bottom. It will be ready in 10–15 minutes. Serves 80.

✁ BREAD, BUNS, AND PASTRIES ✁

LEAH'S CINNAMON ROLLS

1 cup dry yeast
15 cups water
1¾ cups butter or margarine
8 cups sugar

6 cups shortening
¾ cup salt
18 eggs
40 cups boiled milk
Flour

Soak yeast in the 15 cups water. Beat margarine or butter, sugar, shortening, salt, and eggs till nice and fluffy. Add water with yeast and scalded milk, then enough flour to make a soft dough that's not runny but firm enough to handle. Let rise 1 hour. Cut dough into 2-pound pieces. Let rise ½ hour from the time you started to cut. Now roll out dough. Spread with 1 cup filling on each piece evenly spread out. Roll up the long way in 1 long roll. Now cut this roll into 1⅔-inch-wide pieces and place 6 onto a 9-inch pie pan. Let rise 1 hour 15 minutes. Bake at 275°F for 25–30 minutes.

Filling:

4 pounds butter
16 cups sugar (half brown and half white)
1¾ cups cinnamon

- -

FAST-RISING BUNS

(measurements given for three different yields)

7½	15	20 cups milk	⅓	⅔	1 cup honey	
4½	9	12 cups water	3	6	8 cups sugar	
¾	1½	2 cups chicken fat	2¼	4½	6 tablespoons salt	
¾	1½	2 cups margarine	6	12	16 eggs	
6	12	16 tablespoons yeast	30	60	70 cups flour	

Mix dough. Knead 15 minutes. Let rise 1 hour. Knead. Let rise till double in bulk. Roll in buns. Let rise 1½–2 hours on pan. Bake 20 minutes at 375°F.

- -

BUNS FOR CHRISTMAS AND EASTER

Yeast mixture:

1½ cups yeast
18 cups water
9 tablespoons sugar

1 cup honey
5 cups butter
1½ cups pork lard
20 cups sugar
¾ cup salt
40 cups milk
12 cups thick cream
12 eggs
2 cups lard
Enough flour to make a soft dough, about 38 quarts

Let rise 1 hour and 15 minutes. Knead down. Let rise 1 full hour.

Roll buns. Let rise 2 hours on pan. Bake at 375°F for 20 minutes.

- -

RASCHA ZWIEBOCH

(Crisp Buns)

Also called "maternity buns" because new mothers receive a bushel of Rascha Zwieboch as part of their gift package from the community.

7 lbs butter
4 cups chicken fat
3 cups pork lard
¾ cup salt
30 eggs
22 cups sugar
2½ cups yeast
8 quarts milk
10 quarts water
An additional 3 quarts water in which you mix the 2½ cups yeast and
   ½ cup sugar

Mix above ingredients with dough mixer for 1 hour. Take dough out of mixer and let it rise for 2 hours. Make 1-pound round loaves (should look like oversized buns). Place on pans and let rise for another 3 to 3½ hours. Bake for 15 minutes at 375°F, then an additional 15 minutes at 350°F. Take out of oven and let cool on tables overnight. Cut up buns with bread cutter and place single slices on pans and bake for 1½ hours at 190°F, gradually increasing temperature to 260°F. The *Rascha* should be nice and crisp and golden brown.

- -

SATURDAY KUCHEN

1 quart thick cream
5 cups sugar
15 eggs
1 quart milk
6 pounds flour

¾ cup baking powder
¼ cup salt
5 teaspoons vanilla
3 teaspoons nutmeg

Beat cream and sugar. Fold in eggs, add milk, stir in dry ingredients and vanilla. Fry in oil at 375°F.

- -

PANCAKES

24 cups flour   25 eggs
¼ cup salt   1½ pounds butter, melted
3 cups sugar   25 cups milk
1½ cups baking powder

Mix together flour, salt, sugar, and baking powder. Beat eggs and melted butter. Whip together dry ingredients with milk till smooth. Fold in eggs and melted butter till thoroughly blended. For fluffier pancakes, make the evening before and let batter sit in refrigerator until morning.

- -

DONUTS

This recipe yields around 400 donuts.

11 cups pig lard   1½ cups yeast
6 cups sugar   9 cups water for yeast
12 tablespoons salt   36 eggs, beaten
6 quarts milk, scalded   18 tablespoons baking powder
90 cups sifted flour

Cream lard, sugar, and salt. Add milk and half of flour. Dissolve yeast in water and add to mixture. Add eggs. Put baking powder into remaining flour and add to mixture. Mix until smooth. Cover and let rise 45 minutes. Knead down. Let rise 45 minutes. Make buns. Let rise 10 minutes. Make donuts. Let rise 20 minutes. Fry in Crisco oil or pork lard at 350°F.

Glaze for donuts:

3 cups butter
6 cups sugar
3 cups milk

Boil 3 minutes. Cool and add

6 cups icing sugar
2 teaspoons salt
3 teaspoons vanilla

Friday Buns

2 quarts water for yeast
1½ cups yeast
10 cups sugar
8 cups chicken fat
2 cups tallow
30 eggs
Enough flour to make a soft dough

¾ cup salt
2½ cups honey
8 quarts milk
2 quarts water
1 cup Miracle Whip

Mix for 20 minutes.

Put in tubs. Let rise 2½ hours. Make buns. Let rise 1 hour and 15 minutes. Bake 20 minutes at 375°F.

Sandwich Bread

(measurements given for three different yields)

1	2	4 cups milk	¼	½	1 cup honey
5	10	20 cups water	¾	1½	3 cups lard
2½	5	10 tablespoons yeast	1	2	4 eggs beaten
¼	½	1 cup sugar	11	22	44 cups flour
1	2	4 tablespoons salt			

Knead dough. Make ¼-pound loaves. Let rise 2 hours.

Roll out and make bread loaves. Let rise 2 hours.

Bake at 375°F for 30–40 minutes.

When making whole wheat bread, add ¾ cup molasses. For flour, use half white and half whole wheat.

WHITE BREAD

2 pails water	2 cups sugar
9 cups lard	1 cup salt
Blue teacup of yeast	¼ cup vinegar
(very full)	Enough flour

Makes 42 loaves.

WHOLE WHEAT BREAD

Yeast mixture:

1 cup yeast	2 quarts water for yeast

2 cups brown sugar	2 cups prepared oatmeal
8 quarts water	3 cups chicken fat
6 eggs	2 cups bacon lard
1 cup honey	1 cup butter
1 cup molasses	Enough flour to make a stiff dough
¾ cup salt	

Mix 20 minutes.

Cut out loaves 1½ pounds. Let rise 1 hour. Roll out.

Make loaves. Let rise 2 hours. Bake 35 minutes at 375°F.

EASTER ROLLS

5 quarts sour cream	5 cups molasses
60 eggs	2 teaspoons baking powder
20 cups sugar	4 cups poppy seeds
¼ cup salt	10 cups jam (any kind so long as it's dark)
20 teaspoons soda	Flour
1 quart water	Bun dough

Take water and add molasses, jam, baking powder, and flour to make a thick mixture. Now add poppy seeds and all other ingredients and spread it on rolled-out bun dough. Roll into a jelly roll and let rise for 1½ hours. If there is bun dough left over, make buns. Don't waste.

❧ DESSERTS ❧
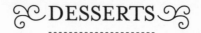

VEISA LITZETLE
(White Christmas Cookies)

12 cups lard	48 cups flour
24 cups sugar	10 teaspoons salt
48 eggs, separated	60 teaspoons baking powder
16 cups milk	

Cream lard and sugar together. Beat in egg yolks, then add milk, flour, salt, and baking powder. Add beaten egg whites at the end.

STRITZEL

Dough:

20 cups milk	5 cups butter (can use half chicken fat)
4 cups water	18 eggs
4 cups sugar	¼ cup salt
¼ cup yeast	Enough flour to make a soft dough

Filling:

3½ quarts of sugar	½ pound baking soda
1 quart syrup	4 cups strawberry jam
2 quarts sour cream	1½ cups molasses
5 quarts sour milk	2 cups butter
8½ quarts flour	2 cups chicken fat
3 pounds dates, chopped	12 eggs
3 pounds raisins	

Mix filling the night before and refrigerate.

Make a soft dough. Then make ½-pound loaves. Let rise 1 hour. Using the back of your hand, pat flat and put on 2 heaping cups of filling. Put the filling on top and lap dough over halfway and bring the other side all the way over. Do not stretch the dough too thin on top. Fold sides under. Let rise 1½ hours. Bake at 350°F for 1 hour.

ZUCKER HONKELICH

(Sugar Turnovers)

Yeast mixture:

2 tablespoons sugar
2½ cups water
½ cup yeast

10 cups milk
3 cups sugar
5 cups butter
2 tablespoons salt
10 eggs
7½ quarts flour

Bring milk to boil. Add sugar, butter, and salt. Cool. Add beaten eggs, yeast mixture, and ½ of flour. Knead until smooth. Add remaining flour. Knead about 15 minutes. Let rise 1 hour. Make ½-pound loaves. Let rise 1 hour. Roll out. Yields 40 loaves.

Miesel (filling):

18 cups milk
7½ cups cream
7½ cups flour
3 cups sugar

Crumbles:

10½ cups pork lard, melted
42 cups flour
2 cups sugar
Cinnamon

Sprinkle 1 cup sugar on rolled-out dough, then 2 cups *miesel*, 1 cup sugar, 2 cups crumbles, and top with cinnamon.

APPLE PIE

1 stainless steel pail apples
⅓ stainless steel pail sugar
½ pound cornstarch
2 cups lemon juice
1½ cups vinegar

Cut up apples and mix in half the sugar and let them stand overnight. Add the rest of the sugar and starch the next morning. If the apples are very sweet, add lemon juice and vinegar. Put in pie shells and bake as usual.

PIE CRUST

6 pounds lard
3 cups flour
½ cup sugar
6 teaspoons salt
6 teaspoons baking powder
6 eggs
5 cups water
6 teaspoons vinegar

This recipe 1½ times yields 80 pies.

SCHUTEN PIE

(Cottage-Cheese Pie)

12 pounds cottage cheese
45 eggs
¼ cup melted butter
2¾ cups cream
2¾ cups flour

3½ cups Rogers Golden Syrup
8 cups sugar
¼ cup vanilla
2 teaspoons salt

Beat eggs and set aside. Beat butter, cream, and flour, then add all other ingredients until you have a nice and creamy batter.

Pour into pie shells and bake at 300°F for 40 minutes. Garnish with nutmeg or cinnamon.

ZUCKER PIE

(Sugar Pie)

10½ quarts cream
9 quarts sugar

7½ cups flour
18 eggs

Beat together but do not overbeat. Pour into pie shells and sprinkle with cinnamon. Bake at 300°F for 45 minutes.

Mogn Krapflen

(Poppy Seed Pockets)

Yeast mixture:

2 cups water
½ cup sugar
15 tablespoons yeast

7½ cups sugar
7½ cups butter
22 cups milk
45 egg yolks
5 tablespoons salt
45 cups flour

Knead dough. Let rise 3 hours, kneading down every hour, then roll out at 6:00 A.M. Let buns rise 1½ hours, then make poppy seed biscuits. Dough has to be very soft. Bake them as soon as possible. Bake at 375°F for 15–20 minutes.

Filling:

24 cups poppy seeds
40 cups toasted bread
12 cups sour milk
8 cups cream
8 cups raisins
6 cups margarine
16 cups flour
11 pounds sugar
¼ pound soda
1½ pounds dates

Steam poppy seeds for 1 hour in water. Drain well. Steam raisins in water for 20 minutes. Drain well. Beat sugar and margarine, rub the dates in the flour mixture of the recipe. Then add the rest of the ingredients. Mix well. Put in cooler overnight to stiffen.

FEIGEN KRAPLEN

(Fig Pockets)

8¼ cups butter
15¾ cups brown sugar
15¾ cups white sugar
32 eggs
10½ tablespoons vanilla
16¼ quarts flour
3⅛ tablespoons salt
10½ tablespoons baking powder

Cream butter, sugar, eggs, and vanilla. Add dry ingredients. Roll out dough into 2 sheets, ½-inch thick. Spread one sheet with filling and cover with the other. Cut into 3-inch squares and bake at 325°F for 10 minutes until golden brown.

Fig filling:

6 pounds figs
2 cups sugar
2½ tablespoons vanilla
¾ jar raisins
5 cups water
3 cups *schnitz* (dried apples)

Grind figs, raisins, and apples using attachment with biggest holes. Then grind with the rest of the ingredients until it's a nice mush.

ᶜᵉMEATS AND ENTREESᵒᵍ

HEAD CHEESE

10 pounds cut-up cooked lean head meat
5 pounds pork rinds, diced
5 pounds hearts and tongues, diced
¾ cup salt (taste first)
3 cups vinegar
2 tablespoons ground white pepper
1 tablespoon onion powder
2 tablespoons caraway seed
1 tablespoon allspice ground
1 tablespoon freezing pickle
2 tablespoons paprika
5 cups gelatin
13 quarts strong soup

Let simmer for one hour. Remove fat before filling casings. Place in ice water and roll till cooled off completely, about ½ hour. Use 2 quarts separate cold water to stir up all the spices before adding the strong soup and meat.

Let it get a little syrupy first before filling casings.

- -

HAM SAUSAGE

(amounts given for two different yields)

35	70 pounds ham meat
1¾	3½ pounds ham pickling (Butcher & Packers #77256)
½	1 cup honey or icing sugar
3 quarts	1½ gallons ice cold water

(For best results use market hogs. Leave on a little fat when cutting it up. Two ice cream pails of the 70 pounds should be cubed or can be ground with ½ screen or meat grinder.)

Mix well. Put mixture into 4-inch casings. Need about 10. Leave filled casings in cooler overnight to give spices time to penetrate. The next day, cook for 4½ hours at 170°F. Leave thermometer in at all times. After cooking, immediately immerse in ice water till sausage is cooled. If using 2-inch casing, cook only 2 hours.

- -

SUMMER SAUSAGE

70 pounds lean beef, some fat
30 pounds lean pork, no fat
1 cup pepper (half white pepper)
¾ cup mustard seed
2 pounds salt
4 pounds brown sugar
½ cup curing salt
1 quart garlic
1 quart water

Mix 15–20 minutes.

Cook garlic until soft, put through sieve. Grind meat twice. Meat has to be very cool. Fill in casings. Put in cooler overnight. Smoke at 130°F for 3 hours, then at 200°F till done. Sausage has to reach 160°F when finished. Or bake in oven at 250°F for 2 hours. Put in ice water when done.

- -

SAMSTICH WURSCHT

(Saturday Sausage)

1 pound raw garlic
8 cup-dippers garlic water
115 pounds pork
35 pounds beef
2½ cups salt in pork
1 cup salt in beef
¾ cup pepper
8 cup-dippers plain water
¾ cup Prague salt

Boil water and garlic a day ahead and chill in cooler.

Dissolve Prague salt in water before adding to meat. Mix for 10 minutes when all ingredients are in.

- -

Bobak

4 pounds butter
4 cups sugar
48 eggs
24 cups milk

48 cups flour
2½ cups baking powder
½ cup salt
1 tub of sausage

Mix butter and sugar together and stir well. Sift in flour, baking powder, and salt. In a separate bowl, beat eggs and then mix in milk. Mix both flour mixture and egg mixture together well. Pour into 2 pans. Cut in 2-inch pieces of homemade sausage and put about eight pieces in each pan. Bake 30 minutes at 325°F.

- -

Hutterite Hamburgers

½ loaf of bread
½ cup milk
2 quarts eggs
1 fist salt
Small fist pepper

2 cups flour
2 gallons pork
½ gallon beef
4 big onions

Combine bread, milk, eggs, salt, pepper, and flour. Add meat and onions. Mix well. Shape into patties and fry.

- -

Hutterite "Kentucky Fried" Chicken

2 eggs
1 cup milk
6 cups flour
½ cup salt
½ teaspoon sage
2 tablespoons meat tenderizer
1 teaspoon curry

¼ cup pepper
1 teaspoon onion salt
1 teaspoon turmeric
½ teaspoon ground cloves
½ teaspoon garlic powder
1 teaspoon dry mustard

Beat a couple of eggs and mix with one cup of milk. Dip chicken in this and then in flour mixture. Bake at 300°F for 30 minutes. Then fry in goose fat in deep fryer until golden brown on both sides.

- -

CHICKEN GRAVY

4 quarts milk
1 cup flour
1 cup mushroom base

½ cup chicken base
1 teaspoon salt

- -

STUFFING FOR CHICKENS

10 big onions
4 tablespoons poultry seasoning
8 cups chopped celery
2 pounds butter
6 tablespoons salt
6 tablespoons pepper
6 loaves of bread

Fry onions in butter until soft, then add remaining ingredients and stuff birds with it.

- -

SMOKED BROILERS

Make a curing solution of
1 gallon water
1 pound salt
⅓ pound sugar
1 teaspoon saltpeter

Cover chickens with solution and let cure for 24 hours. Remove from solution, wipe dry, and store in refrigerator an additional 6 hours to equilibrate. Cover in smoker–steamer for 12 hours at 195–200°F. Remove from heat. When cool, place smoked broilers into suitable packaging and refrigerate or freeze till needed. Keep water in pan above fire in cooker to help prevent meat from drying. Use dry wood hickory chips as fuel source or add moistened chips to charcoal fire to cause a good smoke production.

SMOKED TURKEY

Brine solution:

1 gallon water
1½ cups salt
½ cup sugar

Select one 10–12 pound turkey. Inject the solution into all meaty portions of the bird with livestock syringe. Place the bird in the same solution in a clean plastic container and keep refrigerated for 48 hours. Place drained turkey in smoker, heated with charcoal, at 160°F for 12 hours. Add hickory chips to provide smoked flavor. After 12 hours, add extra charcoal and raise temperature to 170°F and continue smoking with hickory chips. Cook the turkey till golden brown and thoroughly cooked (6–8 additional hours).

SMOKED FISH

Filet and clean fish. Mix 1 liter salt and 3 liters water (always distilled) until totally dissolved. Submerge fish in brine for 30–40 minutes and remove. Prepare teriyaki mixture before brine.

1 liter distilled water
½ liter soy sauce
¼ liter brown sugar
½ cup to 1 cup real lemon juice

Put fish into teriyaki sauce without rinsing. After about 30 minutes, put fish on smoking rack and let dry until it gets pellicle. Smoke for 5–6 hours at 150°F.

ᏭJAMS, JELLIES, SPECIALTIESᏭ

FREEZING FRUIT

Strawberries: 5 pounds sugar; 24 pounds fruit

Raspberries: 5 pounds sugar; 20 pounds fruit

Plums: 5 pounds sugar; 20 pounds fruit

Blueberries: 5 pounds sugar; 30 pounds fruit

Apricots: 3 pounds sugar; 15 pounds fruit; 3 teaspoons ascorbic acid

Peaches: 3 pounds sugar; 15 pounds fruit; 3 teaspoons ascorbic acid

Rhubarb: Don't blanch if put in freezer

APRICOT MUSH

30 cup-dippers mush (8 cup dippers)
5 cup-dippers sugar
2 cup-dippers water
3 cups cornstarch
2 cups tapioca

Cook mush 15 minutes. Mix last 4 ingredients together. Add to mush and cook another 15 minutes.

STRAWBERRY JAM

108 pounds strawberries, ground
148 pounds sugar
52 packages Certo powder

Put Certo in right away and bring to a very hard rolling boil with strawberries. Add sugar, boil 5 minutes. This makes 5–6 gallons. Don't cook 1 or even ½ minute longer, even for a big recipe. If strawberries are sweet, you don't need as much sugar.

CRABAPPLE JUICE

8 five-gallon pails of apples
6 pails boiled water to pour over whole apples
1 ice cream pail sugar

Let stand 48 hours. Drain with hose.

To 10 pails juice add 2 ice cream pails of sugar or according to taste. Cook 10 minutes. Fill jars. Note: if juice is too strong, try adding more water before cooking.

CANNED VEGETABLES AND SALADS

REAL GOOD SALAD

16 cups shredded cabbage
2 cups oil
2 teaspoons celery seed
1 cup honey
2 teaspoons lemon juice
2 teaspoons paprika
2 teaspoons salt
6 tablespoons vinegar

Mix it all together and serve.

BRENNIG-KRAUT

(Braised Sauer Kraut)

2 quarts Sauer Kraut, cooked soft
½ cup butter
¾ cup flour

Fry butter and flour till brown. Mix in to cooked Sauer Kraut and sweeten with brown sugar.

This is often served with roast goose or duck meals.

- -

RELISH

144 ears corn
6 dozen good-sized cucs, peeled and chopped
60 big onions, chopped
12 stalks celery, cut in small pieces
24 red peppers, cut in small pieces
48 cups sugar
3 cups salt
5¼ cups flour
15 cups vinegar
12 teaspoons celery seed
12 tablespoons turmeric
12 tablespoons mustard seed
66 jars

Boil vegetables until tender, about 30 minutes. Drain water and add the rest of the ingredients. Cook for 5 minutes. Fill jars and seal.

- -

SAUER KRAUT

50 pounds cut-up cabbage
1 cup pickling salt
½ cup sugar

Fill barrels with cut-up cabbage and salt and sugar. Jump in barrel and stomp it down with feet until it gets juicy. Be sure you are wearing new rubber boots. Stomp it down until it is covered in its own juices. Two people to a barrel. Put clean towels over barrel and set in a cool place to ferment for at least 14 days. Every day push down on the cabbage and if there is not enough liquid, add some water. Pack in clean jars, adding one tablespoon vinegar into each one. Fill with boiling water, seal, and refrigerate.

Make *Sauer Kraut* when there is a new moon, and it won't get moldy.

- -

CANNED COLESLAW

120 pounds shredded cabbage
100 onions, sliced thin
20 quarts shredded carrots

Mix in a big tub and add
10 eight-quart pails boiling water
10 cups pickling salt

Mix well, cover, and let stand overnight. The next day drain and add
10 green peppers, nicely sliced
20 red peppers, nicely sliced

Mix well with cabbage.

Brine:

30 cups vinegar
30 cups sugar
10 cups water
20 cups vegetable oil

Bring to a good boil. Mix well with cabbage mixture. Fill up in heated jars. Don't pack too much. Set aside to seal for 15 minutes just to make sure they all seal.

SLICED PICKLES

17 cups water
9 cups vinegar
1½ cups pickling salt

8¾ cups white sugar
2½ teaspoons turmeric
60 pounds pickles

Boil together and pour over sliced pickles. Increased 2½ times, this recipe yields 62 quarts.

REFRIGERATOR PICKLES

7 cups water
28 cups sugar
28 cups vinegar
7 teaspoons turmeric
7 teaspoons mustard seed
1¾ cups pickling salt
3 large onions sliced
7 gallons thinly sliced cucumbers

Mix sugar, vinegar, and spices together. Do not heat. Mix onions with cucumbers. Stir syrup well. Pour over cucumbers. Let stand 2 hours, then fill.

- -

SIESA

(Sweet Gerkins)

40 cups cucumbers
80 cups boiling water
6 cups coarse salt

Mix and pour on cucumbers. Leave overnight. Drain and leave in crock.

32 cups vinegar
1 cup coarse salt
2 cups sugar
1 cup mustard seed
2 cups mixed pickling spice

Mix together and pour over cold cucumbers.

Each morning for 14 days add ¾ cup of sugar and stir. After 14 days, strain pickles and mixture and fill jars. Heat first but don't boil.

- -

GOODNESS GUTHEIT

(Pickles)

10 gallons sliced cucumbers
10 big onions
15 green peppers
10 red peppers

Cover with water to which 5 cups salt has been added. Let stand overnight then drain in the morning. Then prepare this syrup

5 quarts vinegar
3 quarts water
25 cups sugar
10 teaspoons celery seed
10 teaspoons turmeric
10 tablespoons mustard seed

Mix ingredients and let it come to a boil. Then add to above mixture, boil 10 minutes. Pack in hot sealers. Yields 18 two-quart jars.

- -

PICKLES FROM GOLDEN VIEW

27 gallons water
6 gallons vinegar
4½ cups pickling spice
27 teaspoons alum
18 tablespoons turmeric
22½ cups salt

We got 78 one-gallon jars from this recipe.

- -

PICKLED EGGS

16 hard-boiled eggs
1 or 2 large onions, sliced
1½ cups vinegar
1½ cups water
1 teaspoon sugar
1 teaspoon salt
1 teaspoon mixed spices tied in cheesecloth

Shell hard-boiled eggs. Place eggs alternately with onions in a half-gallon jar. In saucepan, bring vinegar and remaining ingredients to a boil and pour over eggs. Discard spices and seal the jar. Let stand for 2 days before using. Keep refrigerated.

❧MISCELLANEOUS☙

APPLE *SCHNITZ*

(Dried apples)

Use 2 bushels sweet apples. Core and cut apples in wedges (about ¾-inch wide on the rounded side.) Place cut apples side by side on large baking sheet. Bake in oven at 250°F for 4–5 hours. Finish drying at room temperature for a few days until thoroughly dried. Store in jars or plastic bags and keep them in a cool, dry place.

SCHMUGGI

(Pan Cheese)

1 gallon dry-curd cottage cheese
2 tablespoons salt
2 tablespoons soda
Small fist caraway seeds

If cottage cheese is quite moist, use less soda. If it's too dry, add cream. Mix ingredients together. Let stand 5 hours until glossy. Put mixture in a pan and sprinkle with caraway seeds before putting into oven set at 250°F. Stir occasionally until it forms a skin on top. Takes about a ½ hour.

HUTTERITE RECIPES—FAMILY SIZED

Hutterites are soup lovers, especially the women; so much attention is paid to fine-tuning the broth. It takes a keen palate to create a balance between too salty and not salty enough, too bland or too bold, while satisfying all the different preferences in a community. "If I can please the women with my soups and the men with my meat, I'm satisfied," one head cook told me.

Ask Rebecca Maendel from the Forest River Hutterite Colony in South Dakota the secret to sumptuous Hutterite soups and she will laugh and tell you, "One old hen is all you need!" On a colony, of course, it's twenty old hens, three pounds of giblets, a bag of chicken feet, and one great soup vat. Hutterite cooks use little spice in their soups because they rely on the meat to give the broth its *Schterk* (strength). Tossed with a fistful of salt, some carrots, and onions, savory broths are the basis of every great Hutterite soup.

Of course, the family-sized version would be one old hen, which my mom uses all the time. She takes an old hen out of the freezer at nine in the morning and lets it simmer in a soup pot for three hours with an assortment of onions, carrots, and celery. She makes the most wonderful soups that way. Alternately, soup stock bought from the store will also work. When it comes to garnishes, fresh dill or parsley are at the top of every Hutterite cook's list.

ᏒᏇ SOUPS ᏋᏇ

NUCKELA SOUP

If ever there was a preeminent favorite, Nuckela Soup would be it. It is as old as the Hutterites themselves, devised during the time of the Holy Roman Empire. Easy to make, rich, and buttery, this is my comfort soup of choice. Some people like their Nuckelen *nice and firm and others soft and buttery, so how much flour you add will make the difference.*

½ cup soft butter
6 eggs
2½ cups flour (more or less, depending on whether you prefer soft or hard *Nuckelen*)
½ teaspoons baking powder (optional)
Pinch of salt
1½ quarts broth
Fresh parsley or dill

Cream butter and eggs together, then stir in flour and baking powder until you have a nice moist dough. Cut into rounds or use ice cream scoop and drop into boiling broth. Cover and simmer for 15 minutes. Resist lifting the lid. Add parsley or dill and serve.

MAULTOSCHE

(Big Cheek Soup)

I always kept one eye open during the prayer in the Klanaschuel *and, as soon as the amen was said, I dove for the biggest* Maultosche *from the soup dish in the center of the table. No wonder then that I had such a nice set of chubby cheeks!*

2 quarts chicken broth (approximately)

Dough for pockets:

1 egg
1 cup warm water
3 cups flour
½ teaspoon salt

Mix and knead together well. Set aside.

Filling:

½ cup butter
2–3 onions
8 eggs (slightly beaten)
½ teaspoon salt
9 cups bread crumbs

Melt butter in pan. Add onions and then eggs and fry slightly. Add the salt and bread crumbs, and you should have a nice moist filling. Remove from heat and set aside.

Roll out pocket dough on floured surface until it is fairly thin. You will probably need to add flour as you roll. Cut out squares or circles; a wide-mouthed glass should do. (You can also use your perogy maker, which is a good look for *Maultosche,* although the ones I remember eating on the colony always looked like big square pockets.)

Scoop filling onto the dough pockets and pinch shut. Drop *Maultosche* into boiling chicken broth and let simmer for 10 minutes. They are ready when they float. Garnish with dill or parsley.

GRITZ SOUPEN

(Buckwheat Soup)

This soup is served for the noon meal on Thursdays in many colonies. Chopped onions, tomatoes, and peppers are added to the broth in the summertime. This soup is nutritious and delicious. (I am not a fan of buckwheat, but this I will eat. The egg adds a nice dimension and the savory broth my mother makes is just fabulous.) To your good health!

1 quart chicken broth
½ cup buckwheat
1 egg

Soak buckwheat in a bowl with egg. Let stand 5–10 minutes. Heat broth to a boil and pour buckwheat mix into the broth as it is boiling. Do not stir right away. If you do, the soup will get white from the egg. Slowly start stirring the buckwheat mix to keep it from sticking to the bottom of the pot. Simmer 10–15 minutes. Add fresh dill and parsley just before serving.

- -

ROEN VORSCH UND KNEDLE
(Beet Soup and Dough Bites)

Not only is this soup divine, the beets used in the ingredients are the first lipstick and cheek rouge I ever tried. And boy, did I ever look swell!

1 quart broth, with smoked ham or pork bones
2–3 cups beets, cut into small squares
1 carrot, peeled and sliced (optional)
1 cup *Sauer Kraut*
fresh dill

Peel and cube beets. Add to simmering stock. Cook beets until tender. Add *Sauer Kraut* and continue simmering for 5 minutes. Serve hot with *Knedle* and sour or fresh cream.

Knedle (dough bites):

3 cups flour
2 eggs
1 teaspoon baking powder
1 teaspoon salt
Enough water to make stiff dough

Mix flour, eggs, baking powder, and salt by hand or with mixer to form a firm ball of dough. Cut into bite-sized pieces and drop into rapidly boiling salty water. Boil for 10 minutes. Drain and add a bit of butter or oil so they won't stick together. Fry until lightly browned and spoon right onto your *Roen Vorsch*. For the deluxe version, add a hit of fresh cream to the *Vorsch*. I always do.

- -

SCHTRANKEL SOUPEN

(String Bean Soup with Glazed Donuts)

Soup and glazed donuts ... what a delightful combination.
This is the soup my mother makes every summer with her several dozen grandchildren. We could write a book about the happy memories this pot of potatoes and string beans has given us. Of course, the grandkids consider themselves the donut masters and the cutting, frying, and glazing goes to them.

1½–2 pounds smoked ham and bone
1 medium onion, cut in half
1½ quarts cold water
1½ cups diced potatoes
2–3 cups fresh-cut green or yellow beans, trimmed and cut into
   1-inch pieces

Simmer ham and bone and onion in water for one hour.

Add potatoes and simmer for 15 minutes.

Add green beans and simmer until tender.

Add chopped fresh parsley or dill. For the deluxe version, go all out and add a dollop of fresh cream. If summer had a flavor, this would be it. Yum!

Donut Recipe:

1 package yeast
1 cup milk (lukewarm)
1½–1¾ cups flour
1 egg
¼ cup sugar
1 teaspoon salt
¼ cup lard or shortening

Dissolve yeast in warm milk. Gradually add the rest of the ingredients and work into a smooth but fairly stiff dough. Let rise until double in bulk. Roll out ½-inch thick and cut with donut cutter. Let rise for half hour and fry in hot fat until golden brown. Glaze with a mixture of icing sugar and water.

GASCHA

(Potato and Sausage Soup)

I'm afraid there really is no substitute for the Hutterite sausage Samstich Wurscht *to get the ultimate flavor for this soup because it relies so much on the sausage juices for the flavoring, but I am sure other coils of sausage will do as well. In many Hutterite communities,* Gascha *is served for dinner on Saturday, accompanied by fresh buns, and* Sauer Kraut. Fruit Mues *is served for dessert.*

4 cups cubed potatoes	Coil of sausage
1½ quarts water (approximately)	Dried parsley and chives
1 large onion	Salt and pepper to taste

Cook onions in water until they're tender, then add the cubed potatoes and cook them together until the potatoes are soft. Then add the sausage and cover the pot and let the meat steam for about 15 minutes. Just before the soup is ready to be served, pierce the entire length of the sausage with a sharp knife to release the juices into the soup. That is what gives the soup its good flavor.

GESCHTAL SOUPEN

This is an old Austrian soup, a great favorite with young and old alike. It is served often and in two versions—with chicken stock or with hot milk. The second version is called Milich Geschtal *and is the mac and cheese of the Hutterite culture.*

4 eggs
½ tsp salt
2 heaping cups flour

Beat eggs with fork and add salt and flour to make really stiff dough. Add a bit more flour if required. Knead into a hard round and leave to dry for a few hours. Grate with a coarse grater or pulse in a food processor. Place the bits onto a cloth or a wooden board and let them dry and harden. Yields about 3½ cups of *Geschtel*. Simmer in one gallon of hot chicken broth or hot milk for 5 minutes until soft. You can store in the freezer until needed. For smaller portions, reduce liquids and *Geschtal* by half or more.

RUSSISCHER VORSCH

(Russian Borscht)

A nice addition to the Hutterite palate from their hundred-year sojourn in Russia. Brimming with vegetables, it is delightful and nourishing.

3 quarts water or soup stock
4 cups canned tomatoes
3 cups diced potatoes
½ cup chopped carrots
1 medium beet, shredded
4 cups chopped green peppers
   (optional)

¾ pound butter
6 cups shredded cabbage
1 cup chopped onions
1 cup flour
1 can tomato soup
1 tablespoon dill
1 cup sweet whipped cream

Pour canned tomatoes into soup stock together with potatoes, carrots, beets, and green peppers. Melt butter in fry pan, and saute cabbage and chopped onions until tender. Add flour and tomato soup. Add to stockpot and toss in a dash of dill. Heat and serve with slightly whipped cream.

HUTTERISCH CREAM OF VEGETABLE SOUP

Who can resist a bowl of soup made with fresh vegetables right out of the garden? My mom's kitchen smelled so good mid-morning in the summers when she had this number bubbling on her stove, vegetable peels strewn across the kitchen counter.

6 cups diced potatoes
6 cups diced carrots
3 cups diced celery
2 cups diced onions
4 cups peas
½ gallon of cream
   (secret ingredient!)

1 cup butter
1 cup flour
2 tablespoons salt
dash of pepper

Cook vegetables in one gallon of water until tender. Drain vegetables, but save the broth. Add cream, butter, and flour to the stock and blend. Return to heat and bring to a boil for 1 minute, stirring constantly. Add vegetables and serve. Go jogging.

෨ BREAD AND PASTRIES ෨

Hutterite Buns

2 packages dry yeast (2 tablespoons)
1 cup warm water
1 teaspoon sugar

½ cup butter, softened
½ cup sugar
2 eggs, beaten
1 tablespoon salt
1½ cups warm milk
6–6½ cups all-purpose flour

In a small bowl, dissolve yeast and sugar in warm water.

In a large mixing bowl, stir together butter, sugar, beaten egg, and salt. Add yeast mixture, milk, and 4 cups flour; beat until smooth. Mix in enough remaining flour to form a soft dough.

Turn dough onto lightly floured surface; knead until smooth and elastic. Place into a lightly oiled bowl; grease top. Cover and let rise in warm place until double, about 1 hour.

Punch dough down; let rest for 15 minutes. Shape into rolls, cover with plastic wrap, and let rise until almost double, about 45 minutes.

Bake in preheated 350°F oven for 15 minutes or until lightly browned.

Yield: 3 dozen medium-sized buns

Hutterite White Bread

2 packages yeast
1 teaspoon sugar
½ cup warm water

7 cups flour
1 cup scalded milk
1 cup lukewarm water
3 teaspoons salt
4 tablespoons sugar
4 tablespoons lard
4 tablespoons soft shortening or lard to grease pans

Dissolve yeast and sugar in warm water; mix in half the flour and beat until smooth. Add the rest of the ingredients and put onto lightly floured surface and knead for 10 minutes. Place in greased container. Cover and let rise for an hour before punching the dough down and letting it rise again for another 45 minutes.

Shape into loaves and place into greased bread pans. Brush lightly with oil. Let rise for 1 hour before baking at 350°F for 30–35 minutes.

Greipen Fleck
(Crackling Flat Bread)

Crackling is the crisp brown skin that remains when pig fat is rendered into lard. Crackling can also be made from cooked pork or poultry. If you don't have crackling, try substituting crisp, fried bacon. It's delicious served warm, or enjoy it with your favorite jam.

1 cup cracklings
1 cup milk
2 teaspoons baking powder
¼ teaspoon salt
2 cups flour, or enough to make a soft dough

Combine all ingredients and mix well. Roll out and fit by hand into a jellyroll baking pan. Cut serving-sized squares into dough, cutting only halfway through to the bottom. Bake in a 350°F oven for 30 minutes, or until brown.

Poppy Seed *Krapflen*

(Poppy Seed Pockets)

1 cup poppy seeds
2 cups cream
2 cups raisins
2 eggs
1 cup sugar
2 teaspoons cinnamon
1 teaspoon vanilla
2 cups bread crumbs (just take a few slices of bread and cut them up,
    crusts and all)

In a saucepan cook poppy seeds and cream over low heat for 5–10 minutes. Add raisins and allow mixture to cool to lukewarm. Stir eggs, sugar, cinnamon, vanilla, and bread crumbs together and then add to poppy seed mixture. Put in fridge and allow it to set so it's nice and firm.

Pocket pastry:

1 package dry yeast
¼ cup lukewarm water
1 cup milk
¼ cup butter
¼ cup sugar
2 eggs, well beaten
½ teaspoon salt
2½–3 cups flour

Dissolve yeast in the lukewarm water. Scald milk, add butter, and cool to lukewarm. Add yeast, sugar, and salt to well-beaten eggs. Beat thoroughly and add to warm milk mixture. Add enough flour to create smooth dough. Knead well and place in a lightly greased bowl. Cover and let rise in a warm place until double in size (approximately 2 hours). Roll out the dough and cut into large squares. Add a generous dollop of the poppy seed filling and enclose the filling inside the dough, pinching the ends shut as you would a large perogy.

Bake at 350°F for 20–30 minutes. Amazing!

- -

ZUCKER PIE

(Sugar Pie)

My childhood favorite. Simple and sensational!

1 cup thick cream
1 cup sugar
1 egg
1 teaspoon vanilla
1 tablespoon cornstarch
1 teaspoon cinnamon

Beat all the ingredients together and pour into unbaked pie crust. Sprinkle with cinnamon. Bake at 350°F for 35–40 minutes.

- -

SCHUTEN PIE

(Cottage-Cheese Pie)

1½ cups dry-curd cottage cheese
1 cup thick cream, or ½ cup whipping cream and ½ cup sour cream
1 egg slightly beaten
1 teaspoon vanilla
½ teaspoon salt
⅓ cup flour
¼ cup sugar
½ cup Rogers Golden Syrup
½ teaspoon nutmeg (optional)

Stir all the ingredients together and pour into an unbaked pie crust. Bake at 350°F for approximately 45 minutes.

MUES

(White Pudding)

½ cup flour
½ cup sugar
6 cups milk
1 cup cream

Mix flour and sugar with cold milk to make a smooth paste. Bring cream to boil. Add paste and cook 30 seconds, stirring constantly.

FRUCHT MUES

(Fruit Pudding)

A much-loved colony dessert.

⅓ cup chopped dried apricots
⅓ cup chopped dried peaches
⅓ cup seedless raisins
1 cup prunes
1½ quarts hot water
⅔ cup sugar
⅓ cup flour
½ cup cold water
3 cups scalded milk
¼ teaspoon cinnamon or nutmeg
Dash of heavy cream

Wash fruit, then combine with hot water. Bring to a boil. Cook over low heat till tender. Combine sugar, flour, and cold water. Add to simmering mixture, stirring steadily, follow by scalded milk. Cook until slightly thickened. Add cinnamon or nutmeg if desired. When serving, top each serving with a dash of heavy cream. Serve cold. Excellent served over meat or deep-fried cottage-cheese pockets.

❧MISCELLANEOUS☙

TREPFLING SOUPEN

Trepfling *is often fed to infants or the elderly and is easy and nutritious.*

1½ cups milk
2 eggs
1 teaspoon honey

Bring milk to a boil in a double boiler, then add slightly beaten eggs and cook for another minute or two. Eggs will form lumps. Sweeten with honey and serve in a bowl.

PUPELAH MUES
(Baby Doll Pudding)

Speaking of babies, here is the original Hutterite baby formula.

4 teaspoons flour
¼ cup honey
2 cups milk

1 egg yolk
Pinch salt
Pinch vanilla

Mix flour and honey and make a paste. Add milk and cook over low heat until thick. Carefully add beaten egg yolk so it does not get lumpy. Add pinch of salt and vanilla. After it cools, add mashed banana.

TOTSCH
(Children's Omelette)

4 eggs
1¾ cups milk
⅓ cup flour
¼ teaspoons salt

Beat ingredients together and fry in oil on hot pan. Cut before turning over.

Ahlah Messy

(Egg Fries)

Hutterites are big on potatoes, especially fries. Their fries have a unique flavor because they are fried in goose lard. Just before serving, they are thrown back into the fryer to give them that extra crispness. Ahlah Messy are the Hutterite version of poutine. It can be made with fresh fries, but is also a perfect method to reheat them.

Approximately 2–4 cups of cooked French fries
3 eggs
Splash of oil or lard

Place fries in pan with hot oil and on medium heat. When fries are fairly crisp, pour slightly beaten eggs onto the potatoes. Stir occasionally and cook until eggs are done. Can be eaten plainly or served with ketchup.

Beets in Honey Sauce

2 cups diced beets, cooked or canned
1 cup water or beet juice
1 tablespoon cornstarch
¼ cup honey
1 tablespoon butter
½ teaspoon salt

Mix water or juice from canned beets with cornstarch. Add honey and butter. Cook slowly, stirring constantly until thickened. Add sauce to beets. Let stand 10 minutes to blend flavors. Reheat.

- -

LAYERED SUMMER CASSEROLE

Layer a 9- × 9-inch casserole dish with the following and in the order listed:

Romaine lettuce leaves
2 cooked potatoes, sliced
4 cooked eggs, sliced
4 large pickles, sliced
Slices of your favorite sausage

Top with shredded cheese and set aside

Sauce:

4 teaspoons prepared mustard
3 egg yolks
¼ cup sugar
¼ cup cornstarch
½ teaspoon salt
¼ cup vinegar
1½ cups milk
2 teaspoons butter

Bring sauce to a boil on stove and pour over casserole.

❧ FOR THE ADVENTUROUS ❧

SAUER FLEISH

(Soured Meat)

3 pounds pig feet, ankles, ears, tongue, and heart
Water to cover
1 additional cup water
1 cup vinegar
2 tablespoons salt
1 teaspoon pickling spice

Place pig feet, ankles, ears, tongue, and heart into a pot. Add water to cover and bring to a boil, skimming foam from time to time. Cook over low heat till tender. Cool for a few hours, then drain. Combine liquid with 1 cup water, vinegar, salt, and pickling spice. Bring to a boil and simmer 5 minutes. Pour over meat in jars. Cool and refrigerate. Serve cold with fries.

ZITELA

(Jellied Pigs Feet)

2½ pounds pigs feet
1 small onion
1 carrot
1 stalk celery
2 bay leaves
Cold water
Salt, pepper, and nutmeg to taste

Place clean pigs feet, vegetables, and bay leaves into a 4-quart soup pot. Add water and simmer, covered, for 4 hours or until meat falls off the bones. Remove and discard bones and vegetables. Reserve liquid, meat, and rind parts; add salt, pepper, and nutmeg. Place chopped meat and rind into a mold or cake pan. Pour liquid over it. Chill to set. Serve with vinegar or lemon juice. Excellent served with fried potatoes, sliced raw onion, and fresh bread.

Hutterite Glossary

Abwärterin	"one who waits on you" A woman who looks after a new mother during the first 6 weeks after a baby's birth.
Ankela (Ankelen, pl.)	grandmother
Basel	aunt or a title used to show respect
Bauch	belly
Brot	bread
Bruc	colonies in Moravia
Bruderhofs	communal colonies
Buah (Buehm, pl.)	unmarried young man who has come of age, 15 years and over
Dariusleut	the moderate of the three sects of the Hutterites
Dien (Dienen, pl.)	unmarried young woman who has come of age, 15 years and over
Die Wuchen	a 6-week period of special treatment extended to a woman after the birth of each child.
Drah (Drahne, pl.)	to twist (most often referring to the way the women do their hair)
Essenschuel	children's (age 6–14) dining room
Federsock	homemade sack used to pick feathers
Fittig	pleated apron
Freiwillig	free will
Gebet	half-hour evening church service
Geistlich	spiritual
Gemeinshaft	community
Gonsstoll	goose barn
Gott	God
Hulba	engagement celebration
Kamelah	storage room, pantry

Kappela	small white cap worn under *Tiechel*
Katus	homemade hat with visor
Kittel	ankle-length gathered skirt
Klanaschuel	kindergarten for children 2½ to 5 years old
Klanaschuel Ankela (Ankelen, pl.)	women over age 45 who supervise the kindergarten children on a rotational basis
Knedel	dough bites
Krapfle (Krapflen, pl.)	dough pockets
Kreitertee	herbal tea
Kronka Kechin	special cook for new mothers and the elderly
Lehrerleut	the most traditional of the three sects of Hutterites
Lukelah	"baby holder," a young girl between the ages of 11 and 14 chosen to be a mother's apprentice
Lunche	three o'clock break where families have coffee and pastries in their own homes
Mieder	women's vest
Mittog	the noon meal
Mitze (Mutzen, pl.)	bonnet
Muetter	mother
Neisheerich	nosy
Nochesser	the after-eaters: cook and her helpers who eat after the community is fed
Nuckela (Nuckelen, pl.)	dumpling
Obentmohlbrut	communion bread
Oltvetter	grandfather
Oma	grandmother in High German
Osche-breckel	piece of driftwood on the ocean
Pfaht	cropped white shirt
Prediger	preacher or minister
Reinlichkeit	cleanliness
Rescha Zwiebach	maternity buns
Schenken	toasts

Schmiedeleut	the most liberal of the three sects of Hutterites
Schreien	bewitching someone
Schronk	a cabinet
Schwischem Gelt	prune money
Soupen	soup
Speck Saften	homemade lard soap
Stabela	wooden canes
Teifling	person to be baptized
Tiechel (Tiecheln, pl.)	a black kerchief (some with white polka dots) worn by Hutterite women
Tronk	slop
Trosten	to comfort
Unfrieden	out of peace with the church
Usten	Easter
Verstont	understanding
Vetter	uncle
Voter	father
Wannick	jacket for women
Weihnachtsgeschenk	Christmas goods
Weinzedel	farm steward
Wieberwogen	women's wagon
Wiet	financial manager
Zomstelln	uniting in marriage
Zu Die Leit	"to the people," transition to adulthood
Zullbrueder	respected senior decision makers on the colony

BIBLIOGRAPHY

Forest River Hutterian Brethren. *Pots of Gold from Hutterian Kitchens*
    (Fordville, North Dakota: Forest River Hutterian Brethren,1984)
Gross, Paul S. *The Hutterite Way* (Freeman, South Dakota: Freeman
    Publishing Company, 1965)
Hostetler, John A. *Hutterite Society* (Baltimore: The John Hopkins
    University Press, 1997)
Hutterian Brethren, The. *Treasures of Time*, XVIII (Elie, Manitoba:
    R.M. of Cartier, 1985)
Global Anabaptist Mennonite Encyclopedia Online (http://gameo.org)
Janzen, Rod and Max Stanton. *The Hutterites in North America*
    (Baltimore: The Johns Hopkins University Press, 2010)
Peters, Victor. *All Things Common: The Hutterian Way of Life*
    (Minneapolis: University of Minnesota Press, 1965)
Walter, Judy. *At Home in the Kitchen: Mennonite, Hutterite and Amish
    Style Cooking* (Lethbridge, Alberta: At Home in the Kitchen, 2009)

ACKNOWLEDGMENTS

I am indebted to the head cooks at the various Hutterite colonies for giving freely of their time, for being so forthcoming with information, and for treating me as one of their own. I am equally thankful to the colony women who enfolded me into their lives and work cycles and who with good humor concluded that I was not worth *eh hayler* (the money) when it came to manual labor!

To my amazing sister, Genie Schaap, who traveled with me to many of the colonies and who stepped in to remind my incurably curious Hutterite subjects that I was there to interview *them* and not they *me*. I am so lucky to have you for a sister!

To Arvel Gray, my editor and friend, for her help in kneading and shaping the manuscript, and for getting up with me at the unearthly hour of 5:00 a.m. to bake pies with the colony women.

To Rick Broadhead, my agent, for taking me on, opening doors, and finding me a great publisher.

To Andrea Magyar, business and lifestyle publishing director at Penguin, for her patience and invaluable feedback with the manuscript.

To the rest of my wonderful team at Penguin: Sandra Tooze, my production editor; Chrystal Kocher, production coordinator; Rachel Brown, editorial assistant; Janette Thompson (Jansom), for her interior design and formatting work; copyeditor Patricia Jones; and proofreader Claudia Forgas.

To my mother, Mary Dornn, for your love and support, and for creating smaller versions of Hutterite favorites.

To Paul Wipf from Viking Colony, for being such an invaluable resource and a wonderful Hutterite brother.

To Tony Waldner from Forest River Colony for his expertise with the Hutterisch translations. Readers will notice a slight change from the way some Hutterisch words were spelled in *I Am Hutterite*. Since then, a committee has set out to formalize the spelling of our oral language.

The photograph of the beautiful Hutterite ceramic plate on page 1 is courtesy of Dr. Anna Ridovics, curator of the Hungarian National Museum Ceramic Collection. Today entire factories like this one in Hungary (www.habankeramia.com) are dedicated to recreating original works by Hutterite potters.

Last but not least, to the light of my life, my son, Levi.